GH00870740

SNOW

lit rev

4

SPRING 2016

A·B

TAKASHI HIRAIDE

translated from the Japanese by

KUMIKO KIUCHI

ON KAWARA AS LANGUAGE [1]

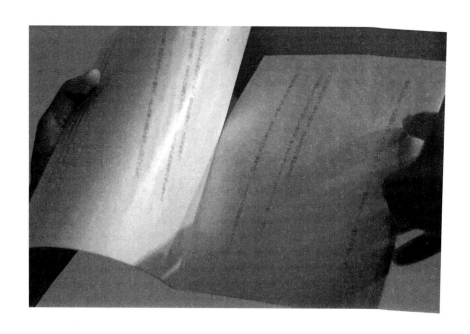

1. The Beginning

The approach I have here to the art of On Kawara can be said to be a little off the beaten track of contemporary art theory, in that I propose to expand some reflections on the theme "On Kawara as Language".

First we have to remove some potential misunderstandings that can arise from this theme. In what way does "language" invade the world of "materials" such as screens and painting tools? In what way does "language" liberate "materials"? In other words, how can a painter get "language" on his side? It seems that all these simple questions are still being asked in different forms in different situations in the world of art today. However, all these questionings treat "language" only as something different from the morphologic substance or visual illusion attributed to art.

Here, I do not take the view that presupposes these artistic styles or genres as readymades, nor do I seek to question and speak of "language" only as a standard by which to measure how much an artwork deviates from given standards. Such a manner of questioning would only end up classifying different styles based on different levels of materials. Assigning unilaterally such a role to "language" is ultimately bound to trigger its retribution.

As for the stupidity of such a materialist view, the view that treats "language" only as material, it is sufficient to take a brief look back at the revolutionary significance of art since the beginning of the twentieth century, which reveals that the exploration of the "material" world should necessarily also be that of the "language" world. We have to understand that these two worlds are not separate; they exist not independently of each other but are intermingled. We have to recognize afresh that, in our twentieth-century human society, the relationship between "thing" and "language" lies in the process of radically losing their basic one-to-one correspondence.

In our century, "language" does not display its capacity to refer to "thing" as directly as it did before. Rather, "language" finds itself in a constant state of madness in signification. Even before "language" refers to "thing", it appears as if "thing" itself uttered a language yet to be articulated as such. Moreover, "thing" and "language", while weakening each other, come to simulate necessity, which turns into a habitual environment surrounding us with constraints. In other words, "thing" and "language" conspire together to place restraints on human beings.

For example, over the course of art history since Dada and Marcel Duchamp, such an agitating and complicit relationship between "thing" and "language" has progressed even more dramatically, against which several bold counterattacks have been made. One can say that in art the relationship between "thing" and "language" has progressed in parallel to the relationship between "thing" and "image", in that the question of "image" has also been subjected to the most complicated agitation. There is an irreversible situation going on: unending displacement, repetition, and multiplication of "image" or, in a word, its pluralization. We are no longer able to believe that image is identical and static at any moment.

Behind this lies the culture and social system resulting from the complicity between "thing" and "image" and, in parallel, the complicity between "thing" and "language". There are also several instinctive rebellions by artists against these habitual necessities which, needless to say, in this case include the methods and the presence of their predecessors in art.

When one looks at Dada as one source of contemporary art from the viewpoint of "language", one can see two aspects of the word "language": semantic content and appearance (as phoneme and also as the pictorial shape of a letter). This also illuminates that the work of Dadaists was to disconnect these two aspects and liberate "language" from meaning. This is what we usually call the destruction of language.

Dadaists sought to disconnect themselves from the art of the past. They regarded language as the foundation of 19th century rationalism, a foundation that, needing to be replaced by human existence, they began dismantling. However, in linguistic terms this was the destruction of codes. Codes are the mechanism that not only enable the construction of a message but also highlight every element in a message so as to elicit meaning. In other words, when a word has its code destructed, it loses its referential function, its capacity to refer to a "thing". Thus the attempt to liberate form from meaning eventually leads to the losing sight of the object it seeks to destruct. Though their methods of destruction first came as a shock and a marvel, many of them inevitably soon lost their impact.

Yet, we cannot deny that Dada was truly remarkable in that it discovered a hinge connecting semantic content with a pictorial shape of letters and deliberately took it off—this was Dada's precious "moment".

So far I have taken a rather long preamble for a beginning. Now, I am about to enter the world of On Kawara.

On Kawara has been discussed in the context of post-Dada and post-Duchamp; he has been treated as one typical example of the conceptual art movement of the 1960s and also as one ultimate height reached by the New York School up till today. It is not only the artist who has to continue his "rebellion" against the way his art is outlined and anchored by the history of art, from the inherent validity imposed by it.

I am not sure if my approach is to be one of these rebellions but I would like to have some thoughts through "language", the *matière* I have been engaged with in literary forms such as poetry and prose. For this purpose, I have to examine the "moment" in which On Kawara in his methods lets go of conventional art based on visual illusion. I have to look very hard at his grammar of subjective displacement, which he draws into his methods in order to keep the "moment" alive.

This displacement does not mean a chronological displacement such as a change in style, because it is happening in his work all the time. The artist lives the "moment" and, with some time-lag, the viewer also begins to live it. Such a "moment" differs greatly from the innovative and ground-breaking and therefore precious "moments" invented by certain artworks in the past. Yet, all these "moments" are the same "moment" in that they constitute the main body that has been and will be renewed.

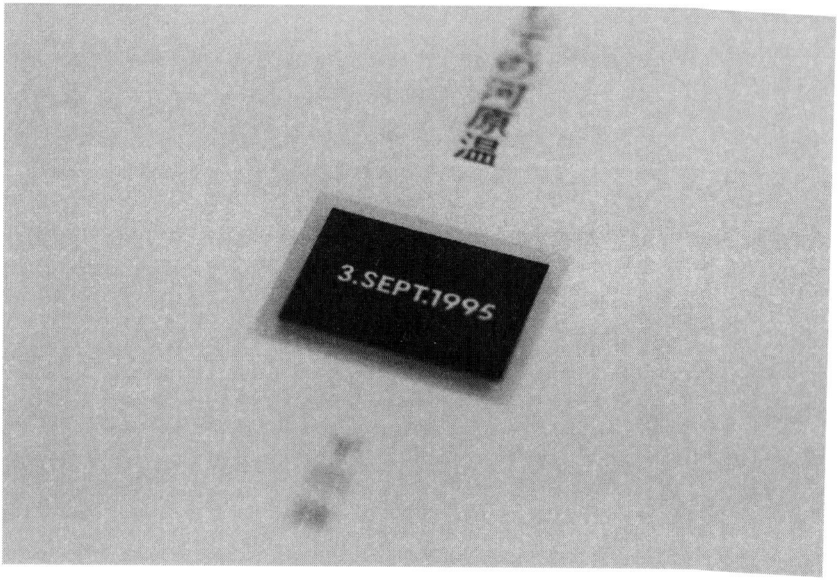
3.SEPT.1995

2. CHRONOLOGY

On Kawara first appeared in the Japanese art world in 1952 at the age of nineteen. Works dating from that year are *Thinking Man*, *Butcher's Wife*, and *Smallpox*. It is incredible that a newcomer to the art world should have created these pieces with such premeditated construction, a strong touch of malice and humour, and deep reflection on themes that can only arise from serious consideration of the circumstances of the time.[2]

People often speak of the two pencil drawings on paper, THE BATH-ROOM series, and EVENTS IN A WAREHOUSE series, from 1954, which are said never to lose their mythical influence.

There are other important works from this period but at first glance none of them appears to be created by the artist of "Date Paintings".

In 1959, On Kawara left Japan and settled in Mexico for four years. According to his own account, his works from this period are an "extension" of his earlier works in Japan, which he later "abandoned". In his exhibition in Stockholm in 1980, some of his drawings from his year in Paris—he had moved from Mexico to Paris after a stay in New York in-between—were displayed. These drawings can be seen as a prelude to his "Date Paintings": *Nothing, Something, Everything* (1963), *Questions. "Give Sentences . . ."* (1964), and *Code* and *Location* (both 1965), all of which are included in the catalogue *On Kawara: continuity/discontinuity 1963–1979*.

It was not long after he moved to New York on 4 January 1966 that On Kawara drew his first "Date Painting". Since then, for the last thirty years, he has been working on the series entitled TODAY SERIES, one of which he painted today in this place.

It may no longer be necessary to explain that he has worked on such series as I GOT UP AT . . ., I READ, I WENT, I AM STILL ALIVE, along with his "Date Paintings".[3]

It may seem tiresome to outline the chronology of an artist who tackles "time" as his true theme, who seeks at the same time to present only the "present" by erasing altogether details of his past from the public arena.

Yet, I have felt it necessary as a step forward in working on a theory of language in the manner of a theory of time.

3. FLEETING "MOMENTS"

In the art of On Kawara, centred on the "Date Paintings", "language" indeed functions at the forefront and in the entirety of his work. It goes beyond the level of expression of letters and clearly operates its significa-tion. Yet, at the same time, the work continues to be elaborately drawn by hand. It is painting as the result of manual work.

What is certain is that time already exists as multiple layers in this painting. Firstly, there is this "language" which contains the time lived by the subject, and the date that marks a semantic content of "language". Though the date may appear to refer to one point in time, in fact it im-pregnates the passing of the time of day. Furthermore, there is another time, which, though attributed to a day, flows differently from the time of the everyday—the time when the artist draws, the time the work of his hands passes through, the time that leads ultimately to the display of the accumulation of the stokes of the brush on the surface of the painting.

In one of his series, a postcard is sent to particular individuals to re-port "I GOT UP AT . . . IN THE MORNING" everyday for a fixed period of time. Let us look at an example—the postcard with the message "I GOT UP AT 9:51 A.M." The length of time passing here is equal to the length during which the "I" utters this short sentence. The word "I" pre-sumably signifies the person making this statement referring to a trivial fact that the I got up at 9:51 A.M. in the morning—a scene from this person's everyday life. One can assume that this statement was made after this indicated time, though on the same day. Moreover, even the time when this statement was made is not exactly one specific point = moment in time—time passes while rubber stamps are being impressed on the postcard. There are also other times—the time up to it being thrown into a postbox, until it is stamped with a postmark at a post office, until it is delivered to the letterbox of the recipient, the time until this friend takes it out of the box and reads it, until the time it is reread, and until the time comes when in some way it reaches random viewers. All these times are in succession. What is crucial here is that we can see clearly all these layers of time on this one very simple postcard.

With these points considered, it is now evident that the "moment" cannot be reduced to 9:51 A.M. The "moment" we would like to find continues to escape through several meshes, through the intervals in the system of time.

The postcards stating I GOT UP AT . . . are sent to particular individuals over a fixed period of time and thereby multiply the number of meshes in a net, giving them life. In other words, the postcards breathe breath into "moments" which otherwise would just be fleeting. If Westerners give the name epiphany to the act of intuitively grasping the entirety of truth in the repetition of simple and mundane experience, then this epiphany may attest to the fact that the "expression per se is not an expression".

By the way, the "expression per se is not an expression" is not just a special "moment" brought about by art but is also one of the conditions of our existence today. This resembles very much the fact that our everyday life is not in itself equal to the time or place in which we live.

The idea that the expression should present the lived time and place in the present has long been invalid. The twentieth-century has witnessed a condition where "language" no longer refers to "thing", where "image" can no longer confront "thing", as I noted at the beginning. It is becoming much harder to find such lived experience rendered in the present only within the medium of our life. These conditions have been ocurring in our existence even at a deep level and in complicated ways.

Then, it so happens at times that "what is excluded from an expression becomes an expression". In my view, the method of On Kawara lies in this expression, accurately grasping the fundamental meaning of this paradoxical situation and turning it into methods, namely the expression which has "exclusion" as its principle.

In On Kawara's methods, the grids of the calendar are not a butterfly net chasing after an insect called a "moment". Rather, the net lets the "moment" pass through the grids. Time itself can never become a "moment"—it consists of layers with overlapping surfaces. By fraying the surface and thus making a crevice in the layers, a "moment" can escape. This "moment" is now revived outside the artist's self and outside the expression as the artist's self.

On Kawara has been working on "Date Paintings" for a long time now, while moving around the world. These paintings visually show only the dates as schematic and invariable images deprived of hot and cold and even of malice and humour, though they correspond to life in displacement, to its place and time.

The repetitive and unilateral image seeks to "exclude" living images, which are supposed to bear rich continuity. Yet, this method is theoretical and strictly rooted in this paradox of "exclusion", allowing us to touch directly on the main body of the images of the world, which should already be excluded from the expression, the central body of the image that can no longer be called image.

4. TENSES AND PERSONAL PRONOUNS

One can say that two elements constitute On Kawara's fundamental methodology of "exclusion" of image in his art: dates and the first person singular "I". In other words, to a great extent, both tense and the nominative case define his methods of "exclusion".

It can be said that such series as I GOT UP AT ..., I READ, I WENT, I AM STILL ALIVE are in the first person, not simply because the personal pronoun is in the first person. Take the "Date Paintings" for example. Although there is no first person pronoun actually painted there, its method and form allow us to assert that these paintings are indeed in the first person, for these paintings narrate "I live (on) this date". Whether or not the word "I" is painted, we can in no way deny that these pieces are in the first person. We should also not miss the fact that this narrative mode is intricately intertwined with his methods of "exclusion" noted above, and working in a way that constitues the mechanism of the work.

Here, I have been afforded one tiny revelation—paintings of all places and times may always have contained personal pronouns. Then, which personal pronouns are to be found in the wall paintings of Lascaux? What about *Mona Lisa*, *Mont Sainte-Victoire*, and *The Hundred Headless Woman*? [4]

If there are paintings defined by the "I", there can also be paintings defined by "we", "thou", "she" or "it". I have been gripped by the idea that the personal pronoun is latent in all paintings and somehow it can be identified. Of course, this is just a fancy because in reality whenever we have to decide on which material aspect of a painting is to be adopted as a standard at the level of language, we always end up with a somewhat confusing discussion. Nevertheless, at least the first person narrative in On Kawara's work is of the kind that invite us to such seemingly unsettling yet very stimulating associations, where the structures of consciousness of all art works in the past are relativized.

In that this painting uncovers its own grammatical structure, it also uncovers not only its own personal pronouns but also its tenses. And here is another idea: tenses may also be inherent in paintings of all ages and times.

In the series I GOT UP AT . . . messages are written in the past tense. Yet, a voice "today" implicitly accompanies this tense and the past tense breathes in an unbound realm of the present.

Peculiar fluctuations between the present and the past suggest that the tense here serves to control not only messages but also frayed meshes in time.

Likewise, we should say that the personal pronoun envelops its own

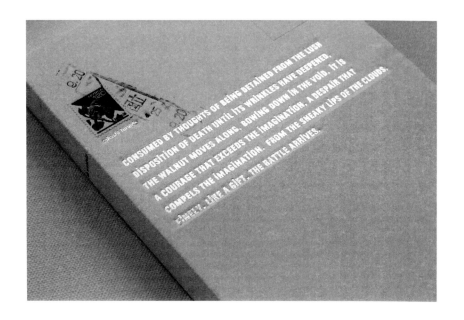

CONSUMED BY THOUGHTS OF BEING DETAINED FROM THE LUSH DISPOSITION OF DEATH UNTIL ITS WRINKLES HAVE DEEPENED. THE WALNUT MOVES ALONG, BOWING DOWN IN THE VOID. IT IS A COURAGE THAT EXCEEDS THE IMAGINATION, A DESPAIR THAT COMPELS THE IMAGINATION. FROM THE SNEAKY LIPS OF THE CLOUDS, SLOWLY, LIKE A GIFT, THE BATTLE ARRIVES.

fluctuations. Can we identify the "I" with the artist On Kawara? No, we cannot. For the relationship between the two poles is in close resemblance yet fluctuating at the same time. It is as if these fluctuations began to turn the "I" into any one.

Now, we must pay attention to the fact that the physical presence of the artist continues to be absent from the exhibition gallery. This does not result from the artist's desire to mystify himself but from what the work consistently requires of the artist. The principle of "exclusion" associated with the pronoun "I" liberates every single lived moment to the outside of the realm of coding, to the outside of the realm of national language by codifying the expression itself. For this purpose, the painter has to exclude even his living body—the "presence of his existence".

5. CONTINUITY IN RESEMBLANCE

There is the series called I AM STILL ALIVE in which telegrams are sent to particular individuals. It could be said that the messages are written in the present tense as if it stood upright like a rock.

Where does this modality come from? It comes from the telegram as a medium used for urgent communication, from the pronoun "I" with its intensity which excludes other nominative cases, from the present tense controlled by "am", from the predicate "alive", a simple yet undeniable content, which has death stuck on its back, from the puzzling fact that this message is sent out somehow, and so on. However, this list is not yet complete. For me, it is in the thickness of the word "still" that something lurks behind, raising upright this rock.

In On Kawara's work, where words are neutral and deprived of ambiguity and humid passions like the words used in sample sentences in an elementary grammar book, only the word "still" contains subtle thickness. This is because adverbs in general contain time within themselves.

It could be that the word "still" may lead someone to misread in this message a sweet and romantic meaning, or to understand the message as a bad joke. Yet, it seems to me that this one adverb elicits a movement of the past covering the present, or the present covering the past. If I dare rephrase this a little, it could be a movement of the dead covering the pronoun "I", or of the "I" containing the dead.

As is often said, I do not doubt that I AM STILL ALIVE is a message bearing a limpid confirmation of the painter's life. Yet, the message shares, in the word "still", in its thickness, in its little fluctuating movements between the past and the present, borders with the continuum in resemblance, with the other world. Don't we hear the message from the other side as if it were its double?

Saying the "I" excludes every other individual from the nominative case, including this single individual named On Kawara. Saying the "I" at these knots of exclusion takes in the dead, the "I", its resemblance. Then, it would not be strange to feel that the dead contained in the "I" or beings-in-resemblance confirm the life of the "I" as their own. Now, the dead say I AM STILL ALIVE.

Hence, I GOT UP AT . . . would be a resurrection from sleep or suspended animation, a discontinuous awakening from the continuum in resemblance. Thus, a peculiar objectivity can be observed through the mask of the "I" which changes like a kaleidoscope.

This leads to the methods adopted in On Kawara's work ONE MILLION YEARS, where the million years in the past and the million years in the future are typed out, showing our/my living time among the dead of the past and of the future.

A newspaper of the day boxed together with a "Date Painting" evokes beings-in-resemblance. This piece of art with a date could be at first just a singular utterance (*parole*). As it is boxed and put in touch with the newspaper as a language (*langue*), it may fluctuate from its first person singular to the first person plural, then to the impersonal and historical pronouns of epitaphs.

Thus, the "Date Paintings" speak: "I/We live/lived on this date" in its fluctuations. In other words, we are seeing with the same eye in this painting what many others have seen and will see across human time.

6. To Be an Exile

As I mentioned at the beginning of this essay, I should perhaps explain how On Kawara left behind his predecessors' paintings, dependent on visual illusion. One can say that this process involves a number of moments of displacement, including his career from the 1950s to the 1960s, his move from Japan to the outside, from concrete painting to conceptual painting. I am afraid I cannot demonstrate this, because his leaps of displacement have been scrupulously hidden from view.

Yet, one thing I can say is that I have been tempted several times to refer to certain examples of Japanese sense of time and space while discussing language and sense of time in the work of this unprecedented artist. For example, I have been tempted to compare the mask worn by the pronoun "I" to that of Noh theatre, or the methodological containment and exclusion deployed by adverbs in haiku, and the paradox of the "I" and narration in the Japanese literary genre "I-Novel [watakushishōsetsu]", a descendent of the Japanese traditional literary styles such as diary literature and essay literature, which was established as a peculiar genre in the modern era.

However, all these comparisons are bound to fail, for these two poles may be connected by their quality of consciousness but not by their styles or methods. How could we clarify anything at all by making a few connections between the "Date Paintings" and certain Japanese traditional styles, when we cannot even find connections in On Kawara's work of the 1950s with that of the 1960s?

Among these three Japanese possibilites I have mentioned above, only the "I-Novel" might escape common misunderstandings in so-called intercultural understanding, if I were able to explain thoroughly its problematics. Unfortunately there is not enough time for that here but at least I would like to outline how fundamentally different the "I-Novel" is from the "Ich-Roman" in these problematics.

The genre "I-Novel" derives from a traditional Japanese sense of time and nature. taking the form of the novel. It became popular in the 1920s, characterizing our spiritual climate of modern and contemporary Japan. Its intention is to depict the author's private life as it is, and because of this pursuit of realism without deceit or making up, such authors sometimes find themselves in the subversive state of having to act out and display their lives according to their novels, and that tortuous feelings towards others have been plotted. Furthermore, when depiction goes beyond its realistic equilibrium, it may distort language in mannerist ways and eventually end up obscuring the subject to the extent that it loses a balance of meaning when the "I" is uttered.

This aspect of the "I-Novel" characterizes the way the Japanese deal with the "I", the way the subject is submerged in the depiction of nature and of everyday life. On the other hand, this genre invented a way to deal with transcendent matters such as death, universe, and nature, hidden within everyday life, while still seated in the everyday. On the positive side, the "I-Novel" is concerned in a minute way with an important theme: how to vanish the "I" as opposed to universe and nature. In certain kinds of "I-Novels", though not too many, the vanishing of the "I" does take place, which in a peculiar way corresponds with themes in works by Franz Kafka and Robert Musil.

Yet, the "I-Novel" has conventionally been treated as a kind of sloppy naturalism in which the "I" arbitrarily exposes itself; this literary genre has even become the negative representation of the Japanese humid climate, which somehow has to be overcome by Western intellectualism. However, the fact is that the "I-Novel" is in the mode of doubling. It impregnates the crises of subject to such an extent as to have no precedents, and for this reason, it is treated as a natural climate to be denied and overcome.

Since On Kawara chose to become an exile at several levels at the same time around 1960, he has been a refuser of and absentee from postwar Japan, a Japanese sense of beauty and the spiritual climate of the Japanese art world akin to the "I-Novel", which he continues to this day to do with such surprising tenacity. Unlike many Japanese artists living in Japan who are content with self-duplicating the spiritual climate of the "I-Novel", it seems to me that On Kawara has never ceased to be in fundamental contact with its true theme—the vanishing (or flickering) of the "I", how to make the "I" vanish (or flicker) as opposed to universe and nature.

The "Date Paintings" are painted in the language used in the place where the artist happens to be. If the artist is in Köln, he paints in the manner of the German calendar. What about his stay in Japan? As an exception, he does not use the national language "Japanese". Instead, he uses Esperanto. Though there are certain exceptions, it is crucial to note that the artist uses languages that are foreign to him. Might this not suggest that he suspends his relationship with Japanese, and in that sense still maintains a special relationship with his mother language, even though the relationship is one of refusal, absence, and distancing.

For example, his work *Questions. "Give Sentences . . .*", painted in 1964 when he began his life in New York, shows how he plays with the elementary grammar of a foreign language, obsessively repeating the moments when he first touches on a language as rules. This repetition is also the moments of his disconnecting from his mother language.

Unlike Dada, which destroyed linguistic codes, this exile has adopted methods of liberating meaning to the outside of codes and of liberating lived time by putting himself in touch with a new set of codes. I can imagine that foreign languages are suitable for his methods in that they are external, given, and contingent for him. This agglutinative language named Japanese, to which the "I" was once connected by an umbilical cord, can immediately evoke its natural climate. Had it been with this language, "Date Paintings" could not have begun.

With these points considered, it is clear that the artwork of On Kawara has accepted in full the mode of the language of this century by excluding his mother language—Japanese. It is a language entirely deprived of being a mother language, being windswept in the world. It is a language as an object to be recognized, a language that exposes the speaker to the crisis of his identity. It does not express any specific inner emotion. Instead, it drifts as an exile through a thoroughly external space, a becoming a language as form in movement, a language that seeds the dark core of matter into space while vanishing the "I".

Here, I am not saying that his work is language.

For it is a painting windswept in the world; it reveals tenses and personal pronouns in art and thereby becomes an object to be recognised; it renews the moments of the identity crisis of the painter. It does not refer to a specific external substance. Instead, it drifts as an exile in a thoroughly external space, becoming a painting as form in movement, a painting that seeds the dark core of matter into space while vanishing the "I".

Suppose that the everlasting dream of art is to eternalize a moment or to shape space filled with such moments. In that case, On Kawara appears as if he has burdened himself with the task of being an exile from this dream. This outsider, absentee, exile from the dream of art has overturned this dream of shaping a space filled with moments, turning it into a series of single moments.

Thus, space becomes moments while eternity continues to be articulated. Now, look at this vast expanse of space as moments. It continues in this way. It is simply duration in the art of On Kawara—the duration of the notion of "moment", which continues its renewal in a revolutionary manner.

14 September 1995

[1] First delivered as a lecture, in Japanese with German translation read alternately paragraph by paragraph, entitled "Shunkan no kakumei: Gengo toshite no Kawara On [Revolution of the Moments: On Kawara as Language]", on 14 September 1995 at the exhibition *On Kawara: Erscheinen, Verschwinden* ["Emergence and Vanishment"] held at Kölonischer Kunstverein, Köln, between 26 August and 8 October 1995. It was published in both Japanese and German in the catalogue to the exhibition *On Kawara: Erscheinen, Verschwinden*, 出現-消滅, Udo Kittelmann, ed. (Kölonischer Kunstverein und Japanisches Kulturinstitut, 1995), with a text by Takashi Hiraide, trans. Heike Schöche. This English translation is based on the latest printing of the essay at Hiraide's own publishing house, via wwalnuts, 「言語としての河原温」 via wwalnuts 07, 1st ed., 22nd printing, 22 July 2014. Apart from the omission of the first part of the title "Revolution of the Moments", no major alterations were made to the version published in 1995.

[2] The original titles of On Kawara's works from the 1950s are in Japanese. For the English translations, I have consulted the following link: David Zwirner, "On Kawara 29,771 days", last updated July 2014 at http://16fdn9ufhox41fwkc1azw8b1bio.wpengine. netdna-cdn.com/wp-content/uploads/2012/05/On-Kawara-CV-2015.pdf accessed 26 December 2015. For titles not listed there, I have consulted On Kawara, *On Kawara 1952–1956 Tokyo* (Tokyo, PARCO Publishing, 1994).

[3] Examples of the works listed here are published, for example, in On Kawara, *Silence* (New York, Solomon R. Guggenheim Foundation, 2015).

[4] This refers to the painting by Max Ernst. Here, I use the English title *One Hundred Headless Woman*, though the original French title is *La femme 100 têtes* whose literal translation is "The Woman with One Hundred Heads".

Photos of via wwalnuts editions by Hiroe Koshiba & takaramahaya

JAMES WILSON

LIZARDS

FOR SOME, the image of a lizard basking on a rock is one of content-ment. To have one's lifeblood gently and directly stirred into action by the loving rays of the sun may seem to represent an unspeakable harmony one could almost be envious of (were such envy not so injurious and counterproductive to such harmony). But speaking as a lizard, I want to tell you just how faulty that picture is. As a lizard, I do not bask on any rock in contentment and, in fact, have yet to experience contentment of any description at all. I find the word "bask" problematic too, for it conveys a certain degree of leisure and levity that is, quite simply, errone-ous—leisure and levity are not permitted to lizards. No, we go about our lives in a frantic and frenetic state, even when we are motionless on the sides of walls and boulders, our eyes almost closed, seemingly doing nothing. In those moments we are sort of frozen; but frozen in a terror and utter vulnerability that is almost as far from relaxation and respite as it is possible to get. Our physical forms may be still, but look closely and you will see how tensed all the muscles and sinews in our fragile bodies are. Every fibre is taut and straining, ready to flee at a moment's notice; desiring to flee continuously.

Flight is the very essence of a lizard's nature. It is what we are constantly prepared for and what we are always seeking. Where we want to flee to, we don't know—destinations don't concern us, flight itself is the goal. Perhaps our distant ancestors had a destination in mind? Perhaps they knew of a haven or place of safety? Maybe it is this knowledge that has been passed down to us, on some biological and instinctive level, fading and corrupting over innumerable years to leave us with only a compul-sion to flee and nowhere to flee to? Today, and for as many generations back as living memory can recall, we know that destination is a pointless and even naïve concern. We can dart beneath tree stumps, scurry into holes in the ground, or slip between cracks in the wall, but wherever we flee to, we know that we are never safe and must always be ready to spring up and take flight once again. Once again and forever.

We don't know if we are damned. But we feel damned and, as far as we are concerned, the latter has a far greater bearing on our ignoble and petty lives than the former. I say "ignoble" and "petty" for that is indeed how we have come to see our existence, but there nevertheless resides amongst us a vague conception of the merest possibility that we possess, or once possessed, some majesty. Our instinct for self-preservation, our impulse for flight, surely that must be connected to some quality or trait that we are proud of and that we want to uphold, maintain and exhibit? Alas, we have lost sight of what that majestic quality is and are now completely blind to anything except our own ignobility and pettiness. We disgust ourselves with our self-pity and cowardliness. We know that we are re-pulsive creatures and we feel constantly ashamed. We disgust ourselves and hate ourselves. And we perceive disgust in the eyes of every onlooker. Whether we are genuinely tormented or simply torment ourselves with our own self-scrutiny, we do not know. But we are tormented and know of no redemption, only a crazed and ceaseless mania for flight. Bask! We never rest! Our anxiety-ridden bodies are perennially on the brink of collapse and yet we cling on to life, shamelessly baring our selves to the sunlight, warming our blood to perpetuate our panic and turmoil.

We need the sunlight like a drug, but we experience no euphoria in its absorption, only the endless vice of addiction. To what extent our abom-ination is self-inflicted has long been a matter of debate. But, outside of that, our persecution from others remains a very real state of affairs. There are menaces that can strike at any and at all times. Everyone knows someone who has been attacked, or, if they do not know of someone expressly, they will have heard the stories. Even those lucky few of us who go through our entire lives without being subject to or witness to such unremitting and unprovoked violences are not spared for they must live their lives in the same fear regardless. (I have begun to think that they are not the lucky ones after all.) We seem destined for messy and horrific fates, and a culture of martyrdom has been built up around that. We cling to life, we cannot weaken our tenuous grip on it, but oh how we long for our own destruction! Oh how we secretly desire to be picked off by an aerial assault or sideswiped from behind a tussock in the dunes! It is a paradoxical desire, but we lizards are paradoxical creatures. This lust for a violent demise must stem from such a glorious and inglorious death justifying a lifetime ruled by fear and flight.

It is said that there is one moment of triumph in a lizard's life and that is the moment he loses his tail in the course of a vicious assault upon his person. To shed one's tail is the ultimate symbol of flight, the ultimate symbol of survival, and the ultimate (or perhaps penultimate) realization of the veracity and necessity for our lives being predicated upon fear and an expectation of unjustified persecution. But this one moment of triumph is always followed by immense despair, ennui, and a heightened sense of defencelessness and self-loathing. Death is usually not long in coming to those tailless wretches that one sees scampering with laboured gaits and downcast eyes along the pavement edges or beside gutters and drainpipes painted black. We are shunned as a species and they are the most shunned of us all. Alone and desolate. I hope one day to throw my tail in the face of my oppressor and join them.

VICTOR SEGALEN

translated from the French with Pauline Manière by

ANTHONY BARNETT

FIVE PAINTINGS

MIRROR

*Surprise & mysterious in a mirror without
a subject. On the beyond of a mirror. Magic
mirrors, so sensitive that every Carving on the
Back shimmers through to the polished front.* —

A quick glance at this bronze grey mirror, —from the time of the
Han, —of course I know we cannot call what we see in a mirror exactly
"painting". But we have said "magic" the reflections that this particular
one and a few others reflect. —Look at yourself in this small round
mirror, which is barely able to contain your face, diminished. —It's a
perfectly polished surface, isn't it; of leaded silver hue, slightly bumped,
and soft to the touch: a disc of grey light. Look at yourself: in the midst
of your remote and reflected image, there they are, jumbled, hazy yet
distinct, the animals of the zodiac, divination squares, roses, celestial
bodies. Nonetheless the surface is perfectly clear and polished to a т. Do
these signs emanate from you? No, but on the other side of the mirror:

turn it round: it gifts you all the mysteries of its decoration through a heavy rim of forged metal: faintly, but distinctly, it unveils the fullness of its intimate splendour, which it blends with the reflection it receives. Wasn't I right to say: a magic mirror?

Painted in Blood

These sketches, done with a single dark red stroke, can hardly be called Paintings. —There's no more spun silk, even and soft, nor chalky colours or blue porphery or antique turquoise, crushed. The painter's tool here is not the pliant brush, as thick as a stylus, as supple as living hair; —but only the living finger, the finger cut by sorcery and exuding its colour; or the finger dipped in blood. These are just sketches in blood. Nothing is drawn here in the tranquility of the study, but at the red moments of life. We do not know the nature of the fever that spurted in chrysanthemums. —The wove is at once delicate and severe: a creamy paper, soft, pulpy, porous to the touch, which handsomely arrays the contours.

It is a cushiony bed where the touch is impressed; where the pressure shows the strike of the finger. —But, here! What erupted is dark red, immediate, bloody and brusque! —Like sometimes, in the past, the masters loved to play with the ink, and tip the pot over in order to trace out (or with a single finger, and an unbroken gesture): a mountain, a beggar, an inspirited genius, a conqueror, a limping hero . . . Here, the unnamed painter has trailed his finger across the barely dry paste. But that finger was swollen with blood. Probably his own. There are examples of this. Some besieged peoples had only their finger for a brush and their blood as colour. And all such fireworks are precious. They are painful or atrocious gestures. They are moments congealed under a dark brown mass. We cannot see any softness there: this is painted in jets of blood.

SOME SILENCE

Others have sought through violent confrontations, fireworks, commotions of brushes, chrysanthemums of ink to simulate the loudest noise. This displays only silence. —A woman, her eyes fixed, lacklustre, her eyes blank; a trembling and delicate face but motionless; —a lip without words . . . and even, not even her breath releases her fl-flourish and sibilant vapour into the air. —Far off, soldiers, swords unsheathed, are searching every cranny of the palace. —Motionless, the woman doesn't move, doesn't breathe, and, from the firmness of the features of her bosom, you can see clearly that her heart isn't even beating. —She is seated, *half-clothed*, beside her grand imperial robe thrown there beside her, which also forms a heap of air and silence . . . Nothing moves; nothing cries, nothing grizzles: the soldiers are still searching, far off, so their footfalls are muffled. Not a sound. —We cannot hear anything here, can we!

Oh! It's because this woman has magic powers. Taking in her arms the newborn of Heaven they are searching for to slay, she beseeches him thus: "If you are of the true race of Chu!" and it has to go on: "do not cry!"—and covered him with her discarded robe . . .

And for as long as they are here, for as long as you are watching, —believe me, you will hear nothing. —

CHINESE STAINED GLASS

If some Master-Painter in the China of Antiquity had wanted to do this—don't worry, he would have. If he had dared, instead of silk and gum, and water, to use luminous glass, with colour melted in liquid glass, —he would have done so . . . Why not do what he did not dare to do? A Chinese stained-glass window! The whole antique decoration transparent! Look! Look closely, this is only a hypothesis, but the most beautiful, the most obvious, the most picturesque of all! If China had wanted stained glass in its large picture windows as the face of the house . . . Palaces were built for that! The façade is, in construction, transparent! Between the floor and the roofs, the entire façade transmits the sun; the roof frowns under the summer sun; it completely raises the lid on the shy wintery eye . . . If China had just dared, it might have had stained glass. It had known coloured glass, bluish, iridescent; it had known the fixing of colour by fire; and the stained-glass window is the igniting of colour by fire and in the sun! That's how we could have seen it . . .

This one, among many others: A south-facing façade . . . under the great roof, in the imperial sun: from inside we could have seen this: the sun, striking the flagstones, —but transparent; —a crush of colours on hard transparent surfaces . . . There are contributions from afar, strange, —yet transparent. It is the entire *tribute to Yu*, it is an *audience*, —yet transparent. The beasts of burden have stopped at the periphery and [are you looking for the Emperor?] he's the one who's watching! and the porters; —more to the centre, the [. . .]. Next we are looking, Facing South, for the Emperor—Impossible to see him, because he's the one who's watching it all. All That, in the Noonday sun.

. . . But . . . After that what painting will last? What ceiling? What pride? What man?

Yes, probably, the Masters of China were wise, not to address the sun, scintillant Emperor of the Sky. Nevertheless, we can address the sun. What painting will last? None, except for the ones that follow.

THE SHOW ISN'T OVER . . .

The show isn't over. But it is inside yourself and I cannot let you in! The four seasons have passed, and still you believe in the full Year? or, like the symbol sometimes suggests, in the fulfilment of life? Then you would be very close to the end of life, and old and grey watching this changing picture in the skies? No—If you are a really good spectator, if you know how to see, know that time will skate around you without affecting you. This is the sensitive and delicate point in the play I have invited you to. Know that beyond all the seasons there is one that the play of moons cannot control, that does not achieve its equilibrium at the hour of the solstice, one that no official astronomer can either name or measure. Likewise, in noting the cardinal points, to the Fifth, centre and middle which is the self, the Fifth season has no age and is missing from the calendar. It lives inside us, it faces off ourselves. Even after this freezing yet nonetheless comforting display of winter, —even after the full cycles of the others, it is down to us, really down to us to see it, no longer in the clouds but in the well deep within us. From now on it's in fun that the other four revolve around it, its different images, lost reflections in the skies.

———

In his dedication of *Peintures* (1916) to Georges Daniel de Monfreid Segalen describes *"Ces Peintures, littéraires"*. "Five Paintings" were not included in *Peintures* and they remained unpublished until issued in a limited edition by Thierry Bouchard in 1981. They were added as an appendix to *Peintures* (Gallimard, 1983, 1996) but are not included in *Paintings* (Quartet, 1991) and are translated here for the first time. A colon is missing from the 2004 impression of *Peintures* at the end of the first page of "Miroir", leaving a logical-looking but wrong space.

With grateful thanks also to Xavier Kalck

ARI POUTIAINEN

Two Compositions

Ayako

I wrote down this piano score in 2004. I worked under some pressure: *Ayako* was to be a part of a commissioned modern dance piece soundtrack. The recording date of this soundtrack was suddenly advanced several weeks without my being asking whether I was fine with this or not. So, I had to finish the majority of the intended one-hour-long soundtrack pretty much over one weekend. There was absolutely no time for any compositional contemplation and I completed this sketch within an hour. The final version of the composition was performed by a standard string quartet—two violins, a viola and a cello. The dance piece was commissioned and premiered by Ballet Theater Vorpommern, Greifswald, Germany, and entitled *Gleis Novi Sad*. I named *Ayako* for a dancer who had a lead on stage while this music was supposed to be played.

Although the music is not complicated harmonically, melodically or rhythmically, this piece has become my "Sisyphus boulder": I have tried to reach the circumstances and interpretation that would be right for the composition but have not yet, I feel, quite succeeded.

The string quartet, which was formed of members of a local symphony orchestra in Greifswald, was the first group to record *Ayako*. Unfortunately, some musicians in the quartet were not of the required level and had severe issues with instrumental technique and intonation. I also had to communicate with the quartet in German since the musicians did not know much English. Although I am told that I speak German fluently, it was a real struggle to explain where I was heading to with this music. I just did not have the necessary abstract vocabulary. Time was also short. We had only about five hours to rehearse and complete all the tracks for the entire dance piece soundtrack. Compromises had to be made and they are audible in the first recording of *Ayako*.

In 2012 in Tallinn, Estonia, I decided to give this composition a second chance, as an arrangement for a symphony orchestra. Again, circumstances were against the music. When I was asked to conduct a local orchestra in Tallinn I was under the impression that I was to work with musicians of a relatively high level. It transpired that the orchestra consisted mainly of intermediate level musicians. We tried the piece in rehearsals but I soon realized that it had to be dropped from the program. I remember how some sections sounded beautifully soft and sad, *Ayako* really begun to show her true character. But we never could have reached the level of a performance within the given time frame.

I later re-arranged the composition for the Bad Ass Brass Band, an anarchistic marching band I have played with for almost ten years. This time it was in a different key and employed a mixed brass ensemble of two trumpets, soprano sax, baritone horn, trombone and sousaphone and drums and percussion. It happened that *Ayako* came to conclude this band's second album, *Töttöröö!*, released in 2014 on Exogenic EXOA 61. This third attempt at *Ayako* is, so far, the most successful. Yet it is clear that this kind of music is a nightmare for horns. One should not write for them like this; there is hardly any time to breathe. At the recording session we could do only a couple of takes because the first trumpet player could play the high part only twice in a row. After a take his face was always alarmingly red and I dared glance at him only briefly.

In all likelihood *Ayako* is a composition I shall travel with from one session and ensemble to another, trying to reach someday the interpretation I wish to hear. This melancholic, simple tune is dear to me. It should not be that difficult to play. It could be that the musical concept is yet somewhat fresh or alternative and that this will call for some extra rehearsal time, focus and patience. These *Ayako* has not yet been granted but I hope that one day this will happen.

AT THE FOREPART

This tune was sketched in Berlin in June 2002. It was one of the first compositions that I felt was finally conveying characteristics of the Nordic jazz idiom. I had wanted to focus on this idiom for some time since becoming quite disillusioned with most latter-day bebop-based modern jazz idioms. I prepared the arrangement presented here for the Chamber Orchestra of Groove, which at the time happened to feature a French horn soloist. The Chamber Orchestra of Groove was a fascinating family comprising a large string section of three 1st and three 2nd violins, three violas, two cellos and a double bass. The orchestra rehearsed and toured frequently in Germany in 2004 and 2005. During that period I had the honor to be a part of this sophisticated team. The line-up consisted mainly of Central European jazz string professionals and we performed only orchestra members' original compositions. Together, we ambitiously studied and advanced bowed jazz string ensemble expression. Unfortunately, only a few demo recordings exist of this orchestra's refined but entertaining program.

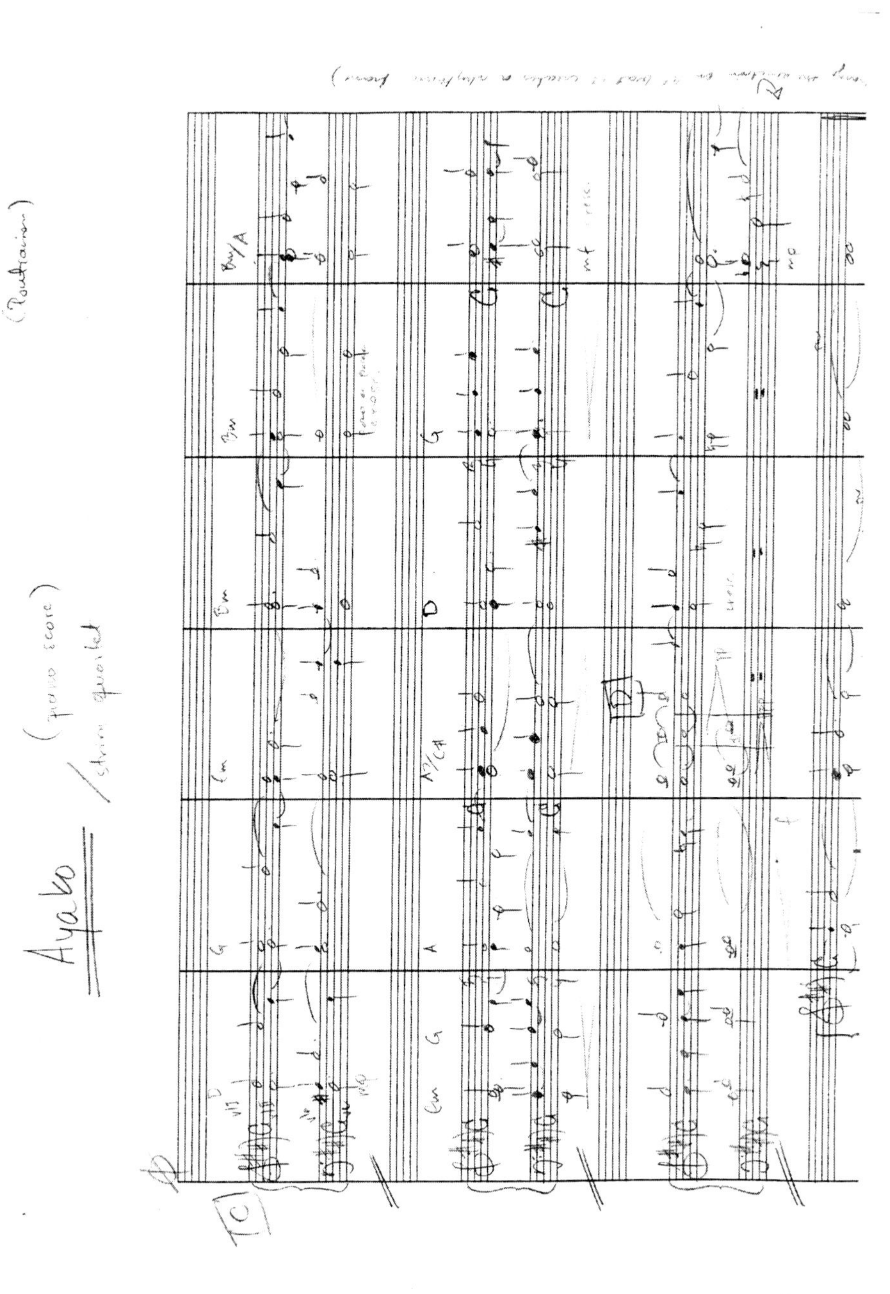
Ayako
(piano score)
/ string quartet

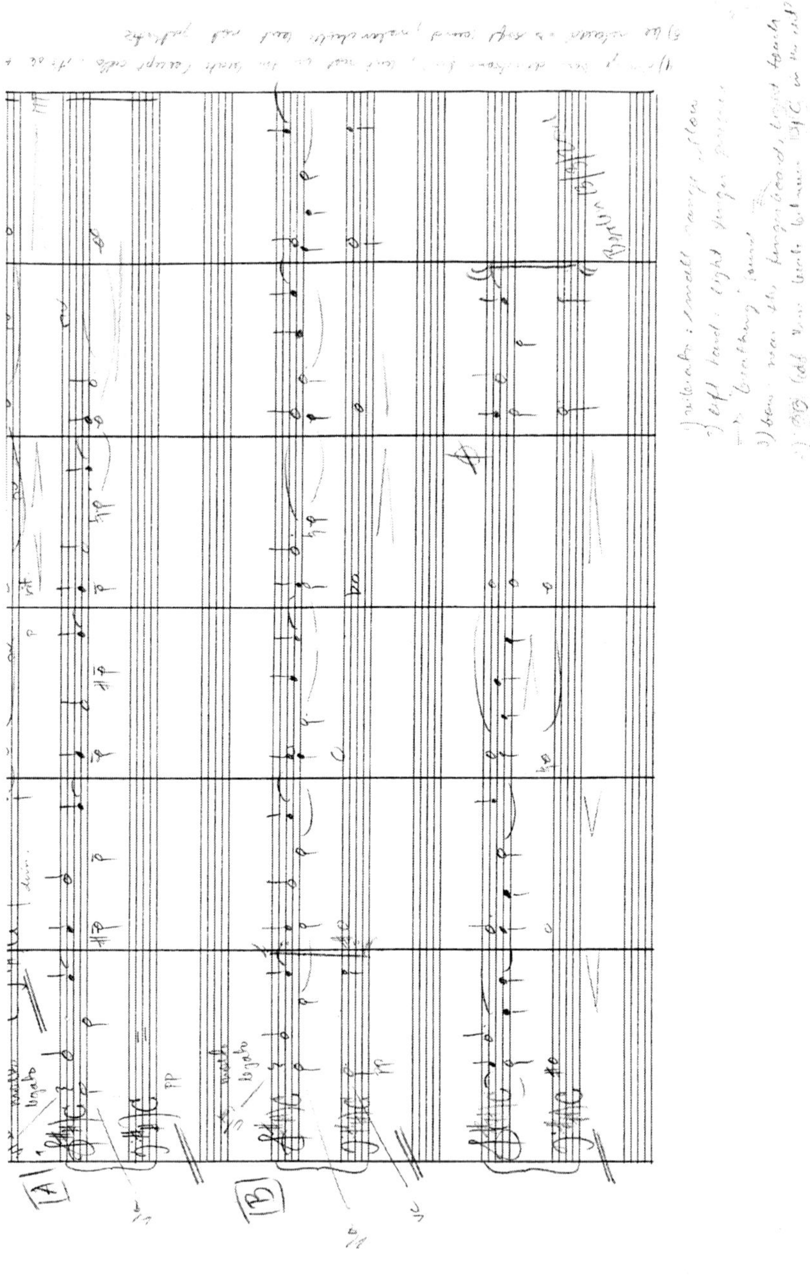

At the Forepart

Ari Poutiainen

ZZAri-2005

[35]

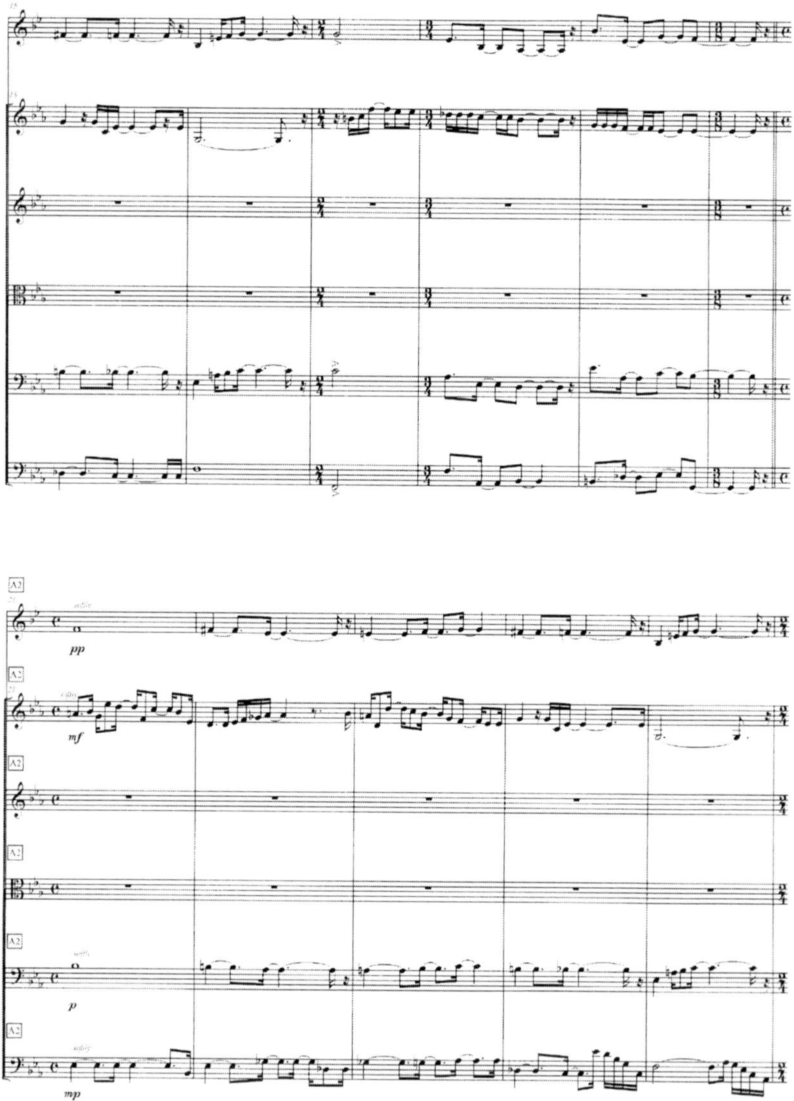
Hn.
Vln. I
Vln. II
Vla.
Vc.
Cb.
A2
pp
mf
p
mp

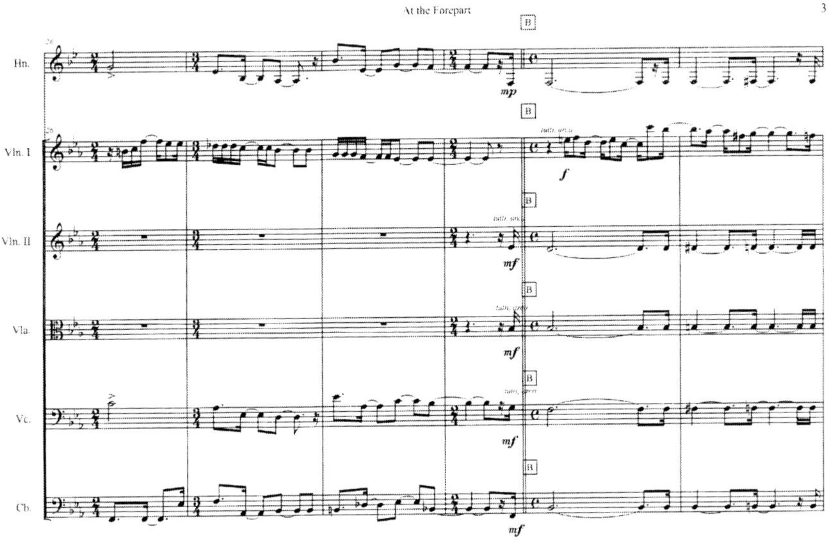
B
Hn.
mp
Vln. I
f
Vln. II
mf
Vla.
mf
Vc.
mf
Cb.
mf

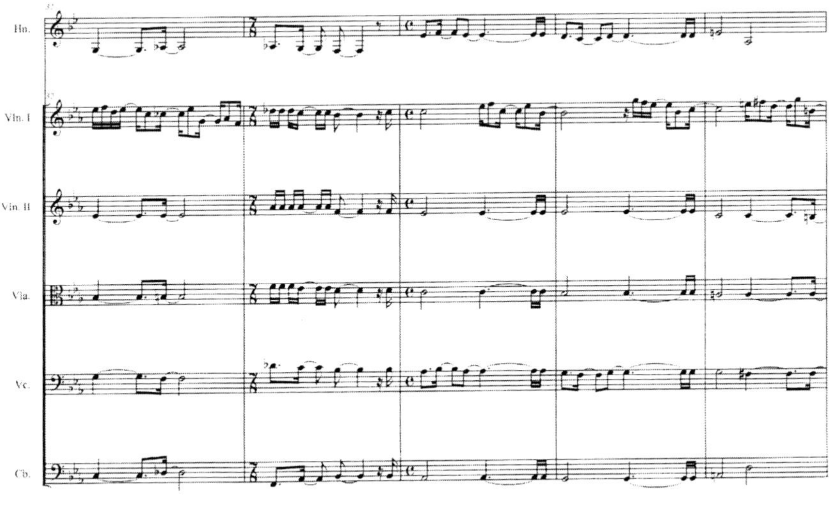
Hn.
Vln. I
Vln. II
Vla.
Vc.
Cb.

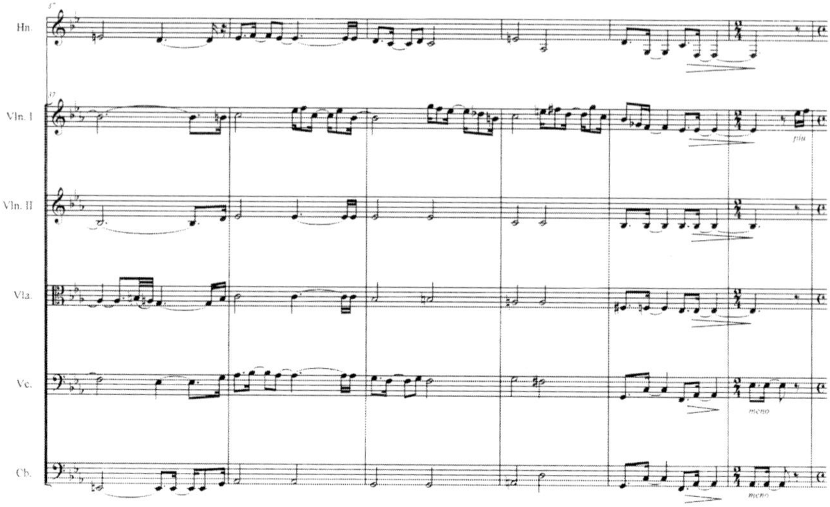
Hn.
Vln. I
Vln. II
Vla.
Vc.
Cb.
piu
meno
meno

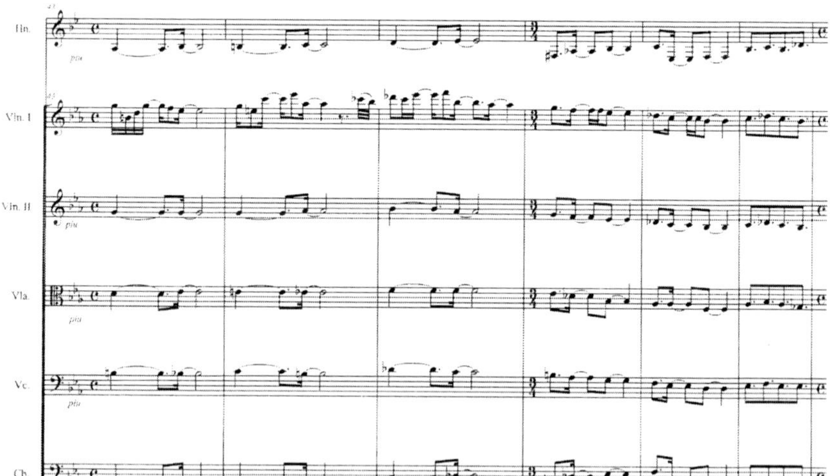
Hn.
Vln. I
Vln. II
Vla.
Vc.
Cb.
piu
piu
piu
piu
piu

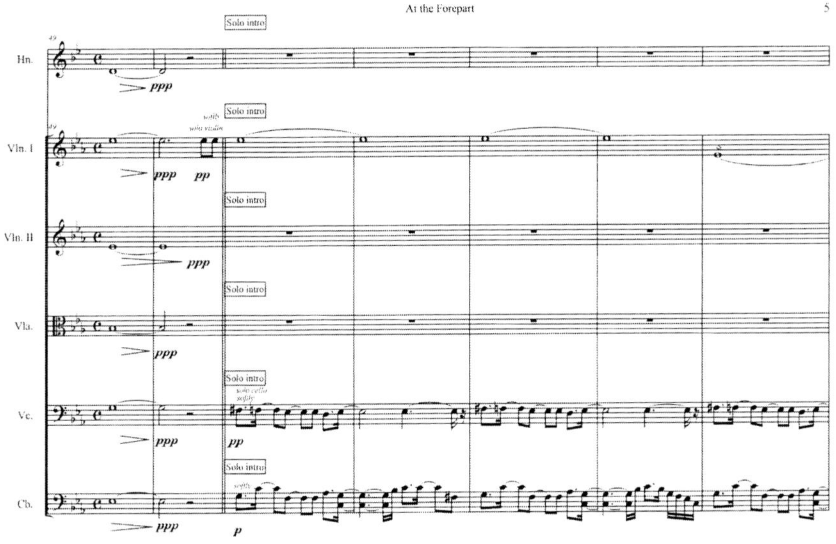
49
Hn.
Vln. I
Vln. II
Vla.
Vc.
Cb.
Solo intro
Solo intro
Solo intro
Solo intro
Solo intro
Solo intro
softly
solo violin
solo cello
softly
softly
ppp
ppp
pp
ppp
ppp
ppp
ppp
pp
p

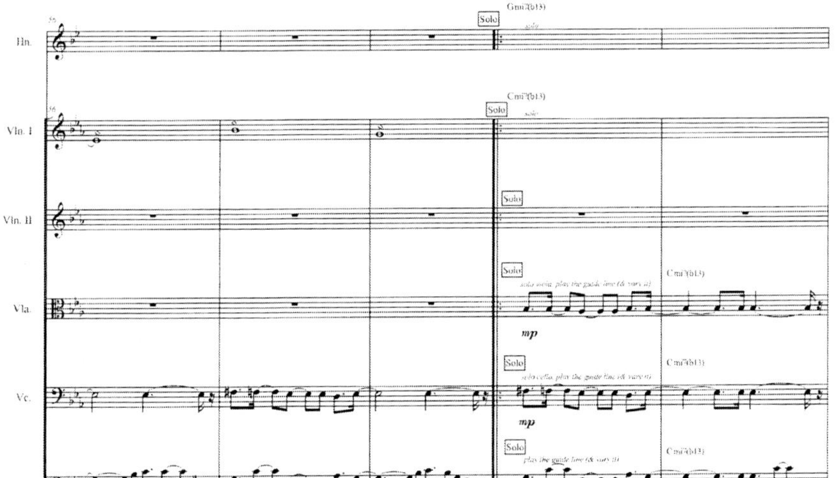
56
Hn.
Vln. I
Vln. II
Vla.
Vc.
Cb.
Solo
Gmi7(b13)
solo
Solo
Cmi7(b13)
solo
Solo
Solo
solo viola: play the guide line (& vary it)
Cmi7(b13)
mp
Solo
solo cello: play the guide line (& vary it)
Cmi7(b13)
mp
Solo
play the guide line (& vary it)
Cmi7(b13)
mp

Gmi7(b13)
Hn.
Cmi7(b13)
Vln. I
Vln. II
Cmi7(b13)
Vla.
Cmi7(b13)
Vc.
Cmi7(b13)
Cb.

F sus
Hn.
ppp
B♭sus
Vln. I
ppp
Vln. II
Cmi7(b13)
B♭sus
Vla.
ppp
Cmi7(b13)
B♭sus
Vc.
ppp
Cmi7(b13)
B♭sus
Cb.
ppp

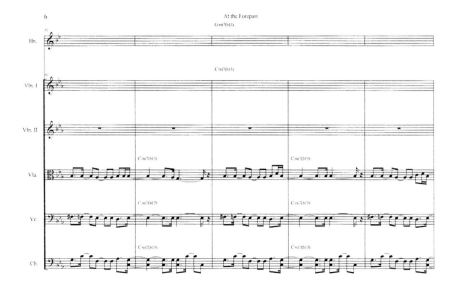

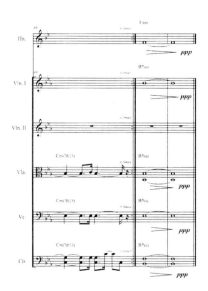

ALEXANDRA SASHE

Two Winter Poems

Winter prevails.   Its mended shoulder
in the overcoat of endurance and clover.

naked cobbles
sadness' ancestry
refrain from the amplitude of their echoes.

Crows' indifference turns into mercy
within the lower
                    atmosphere.
Voices are gone to encrow the South
                            led away by their voices.

The burning years of dust and orphancy
absolved and buried
in sackcloth and ashes.
Seeds sown
            preserved with frost.

Rooms are set towards the twilight
with ink and clocks and the static
deepening pages. The true hand is the rooms' cradle.
The yesterday's bread lost and found.

Winter prevails
       and kneels above us
with a long-held breath, and knees uncovered.
We adopt the unknown
ancestral years, and begin to collect
into its silent vessel
the snowflakes, come
from *Lisieux*, via the *Schauflergasse*,

     And eat our bread at the face of the window.

The aid is hidden and found
in the tear's
centripetal loving existence. Adopted,
our eye
is set aright
   within one and the same
   tear.

Lips are prevailed upon with the fruits
of our soundless winter garden. Behind their gates
we are delivered, — and kneel
above
   our selves,
clothed in the snow
of our naked winter.

from
WANDERING CYCLES

1.

And eat our bread at the face of the window.

Liquid tar covers our hands, the cold memory
takes wing.   A butterfly each
patch of sunlight.
    We tune with silence our strings
    and lean against the wall
    our years' almanacs.
    Time's leafless archives are gone south,
                  birdwise.
Symmetrical traces
of our elbows' fidelity
dwell on the tablecloth,
faithful to their
        patterns.

      Our hand lines
      conform to the warp and weft,
         and –
         coincide with the kingdom.

Leaning back we confide
in the chairs' uprightness and memory
    (tokens of their arboreal
    pre-existence).

They grow
motionless, rootless,
with our arms for branches ;
cushions, conversant with our texture,
keep the secret of our
shoulders'
configurations.

2.

The evening windowscape,
sunset and lampshade
blended within
the roomscape reflection.

Book shelves are
        parallel to the horizon :
fields and valleys
ploughed and lying fallow. –
Among the pages live sequestered
leaves and threads from the paths to the Garden.
        With our white-pure evenings
        we stencil the blank chapters.

Prophecies,
    read counter-clockwise,
yield to the fingertips' (eyes' emissaries)
                auscultation.

3.

At twilight, our face
   of sublimated dust

dissolves — and coincides
with the face of the window.

   At dawn we start our walk
   over the safe bridges
      of our broken mirrors.

from
WANDERING CYCLES

1.

Snow flakes and leaf flakes'
alternating positions
   close and open
doors and windows,

measure the heart's itinerary
with the not-yet- and already-
      covered   un-covered
         distances.

Helmutplatz 10,
    a votive masonry,
sows a meta-lingual soil.
    Trees, liberated from human prefixes,
    encircle with their branches
    our de-verbalized being.

We grow with the trees, within each other,
shed the superfluous pairs
of hands, hemispheres, knees.

In passing,
autumnal clouds and birds
hail and impersonate our
ana-nominal species –
    (in emulation of their passage,
    digits abscise from clocks).

2.

An early morning, a timeless volume
of space and minutes, –
    a deck set outside the over-
    populated eventlessness.

The wooden planks cushion the sunlight,
one's hearing lies safe above the water.

(One walks into an early morning
 upon the ropes
 of one's own moorings.)

from

WANDERING CYCLES

If we stay untouched
by windows and walls,

unleaned against
by backs and bolsters,

unrested under
by bed sheets –
      restful, uncovered by clothes,
      in our nudity, true and hidden. –

If we keep vigil,
counter-clockwise,
awake in sleep,
filled with the lamps'
            meek oily being,

(or if we descend the stairs' silence,
  kindled by light, dwelled
              from chamber to chamber.) –

If we stand still, sheltering roofs,
rained under, snowed under –
    with our hands collected in dew,
    our eyes absorbed in sunlight. –

We will exit the day
through the door of its eve,
effaced from the earth
by its own dimensions,
        and be delivered

                        from Language –

                by Word –

perfecting into a single step
  our epistemological
choreography.

NIKO LUOMA

A Depth Immaculate

1—8

black ink on paper, 500 x 353 mm, 2015

The persistent organizing, deconstructing, and rebuilding of visual space is actually a never-ending adaptation of space; the utopian attempt, perhaps, to achieve an ideal state of purified, immaculate depth.
—Shao-lan Hertel on *A Depth Immaculate* at
Gallery Taik Persons, Berlin, September 2015

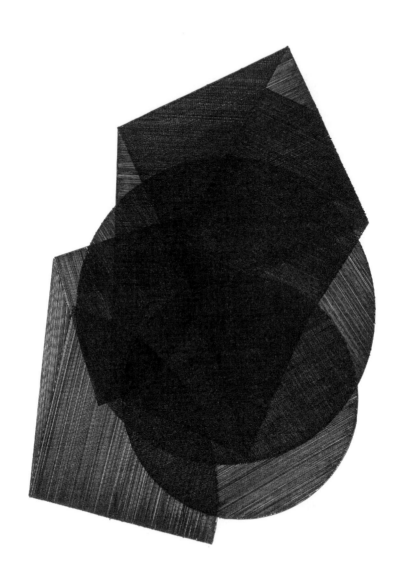

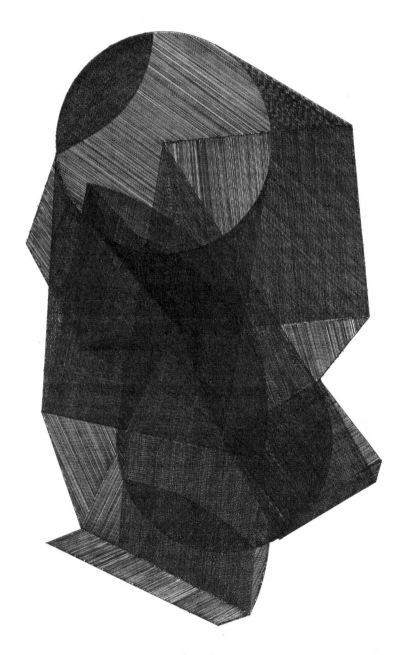

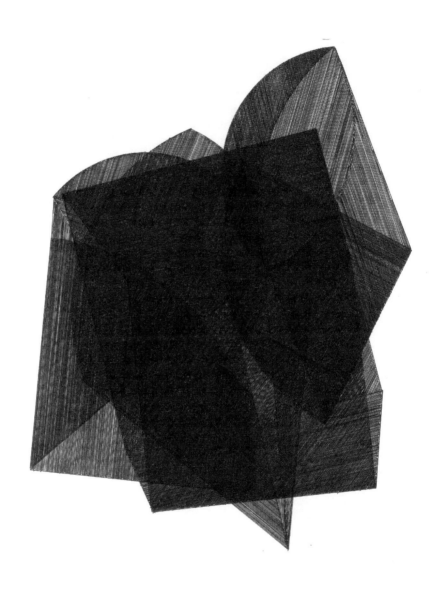

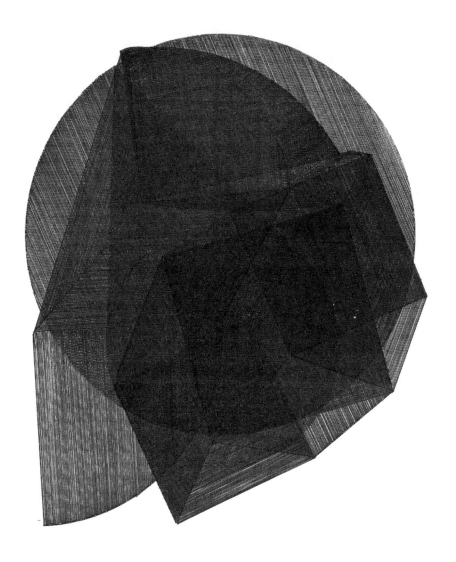

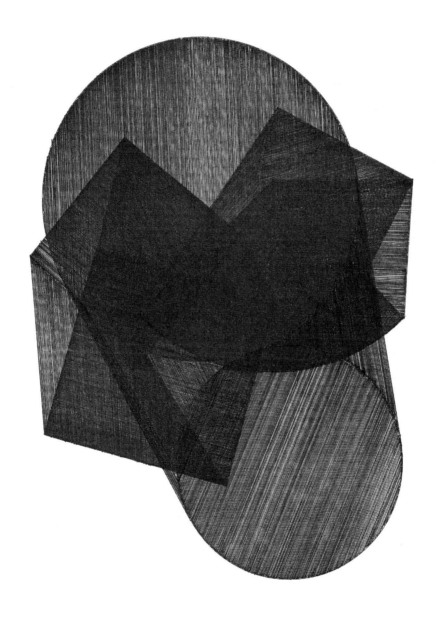

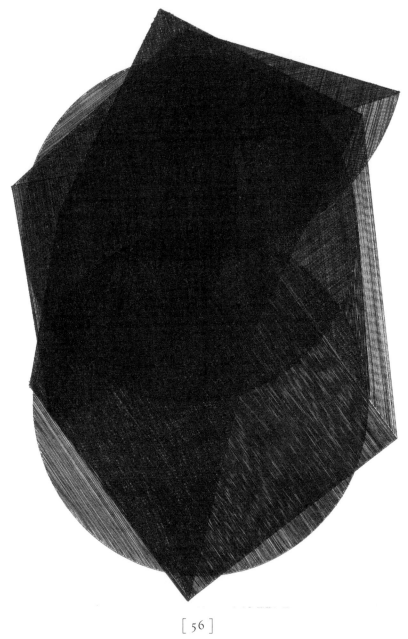

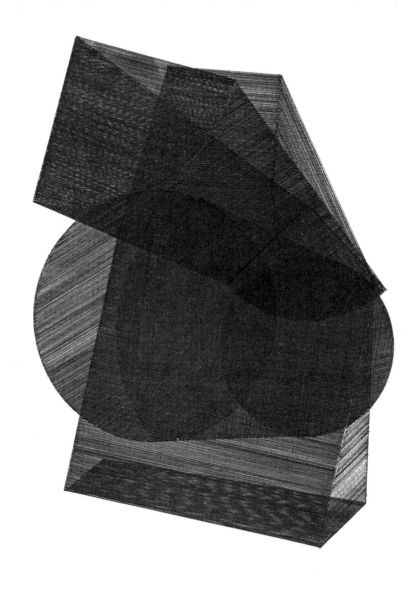

DAVID ROSE

Two Pieces

Folk Songs

DID IT REALLY HAPPEN, THAT SUMMER? It must have done: I still have the notes.

I dug them out this morning, with the rest of my field-notes, for my article for the next issue of *Ethnomusicology*. There isn't much to them, as it turns out: date, map-reference, a few scribbled stave-notations, ingrained specks of ash, and a long piercing pencil-line arcing off the page.

I thought I had recorded more than that. My memory has, though how much has leaked away, how much has been added? It was, after all, a long time ago. I had just left University, unsure of myself, not yet ready to settle to the humdrum of music teaching. So, inspired by the folk-song collections of Bartók and Kodály, I decided on a walking-tour of the remoter parts of Europe. I saw myself as an explorer, a geologist opening up new seams of musical culture, an entomologist discovering new species of folk-music before they died out.

It was an exceptionally hot summer that year, and what with the heat, the smell of wild strawberries crushed under my feet (and tongue) and the flickering of the sun between the branches, I was feeling light-headed by the time I found the camp. I waited behind a tree, planning my entry. The scent of woodsmoke and cooking drifted on the breeze

A twig snapped behind me. I turned to see a girl, her arm extended, head down, smiling up through a fringe of black hair. She showed no surprise at my appearance; it was almost as if I was expected, although I don't recall telling anyone in the village the objective of my journey. She took my hand and led me to the camp, her head still tilted down in respect for a stranger. No one took any notice of our arrival. The women carried on cooking and talking, the men drinking and talking. A few children stared, then went back to tormenting a tethered goat.

The girl took me across to the biggest caravan, on the steps of which sat a man, evidently the *Vlas*, the local head man, who rose to greet me. They exchanged a few sentences, then he spoke to me. I managed to make out that he was the girl's father, and was inviting me to eat with them. I smiled my acceptance.

The meal was quite informal, although I was toasted several times in a pretty potent beer. By the time the meal was over, it was dark. The *Vlas* called something, and several men got up and walked into the middle of the circle with their instruments. Did they know why I was there, or was this their usual custom after supper?

Risking a breach of protocol, I stood up and went across to examine their instruments. They held them out with childish delight; several sizes of flutes, tambourines, a zither-like instrument, and something resembling a ukelele. I thought of George Formby and smiled. The musician smiled back. He even had buck teeth.

I sat down. The music started with what I at first took to be a tuning-up exercise, but which spun out into a long, low adagio, gradually swelling with the low-throated humming of the others. Gradually the music accelerated into a skirling allegro. I drew my notebook and pencil from my pocket. I identified the mode as one related to the Lydian, and began to concentrate on defining the rhythm.

The humming had stopped, but the audience was instead swaying to the music. I thought I had worked out the rhythm, but as I jotted it down, it changed almost imperceptibly. As I settled the new rhythm, so it would change again. Somehow the audience always anticipated the change and kept in time. I made another attempt to fix the rhythm and went to note it down in my book when a hand gripped my arm, pulled away the notebook, the pencil gouging across the page, and gave it back to me closed. I turned, and the Vlas smiled and gestured toward the musicians.

I pocketed the notebook and began to concentrate, hoping to memorise the music and write it down later. By now, the tempo had accelerated again, the instruments weaving around each other in solos and unisons. The audience were still swaying, but also moving their heads and shoulders in odd twitching gestures, always in perfect time. I tried to join in, but again, as soon as I had found the rhythm and was swaying in time with my neighbours, it would change. I was constantly being wrong-footed, deliberately, it seemed to me. I fancied I saw the musicians watching me, waiting for me to get in step before changing the beat, but in the firelight, I could only see their silhouettes.

Suddenly the music stopped. There was a pause as the musicians rested and retuned, then just as abruptly, they started again, taking me, but not the others, by surprise. It was a wild rondo, the audience nodding and stamping along. I was lost from the start, the music being not only louder and faster but even more rhythmically complicated than before. Then both musicians and audience divided, and the music became an elaborate six-part canon, the alternately-bobbing heads looking like corn in a capricious wind. I couldn't even attempt to join in. I was aware of several of my neighbours smiling or perhaps grinning at me, and I thought I saw one wink, but it may have been the firelight.

I suddenly wanted to stand up and shout: "Look! You need me. One day you'll all be dead. Your music will evaporate. I am here to preserve it, to preserve you," but my grasp of the dialect was too shaky, and I couldn't risk another affront to their hospitality.

The music was coming to a climax, the canons winding up and coming to rest with impressive precision. The faces around me were flushed, perhaps with pride as much as excitement. They had cause for it, certainly. Then laughter and chatter broke out and beer was passed round. One of my neighbours clapped me on the back as he handed me my jug, and I smiled and nodded my admiration.

The fire was stoked and we sat and drank. The moon had risen through patchy cloud. The chatter ebbed away and there was silence.

Then a single note swelled up, from the earth, it seemed to me. The adagio began, as before, but more plaintive. It was the most eerie, melancholy thing I have heard. The audience sat completely still, yet somehow gave the impression of moving, rocking together. They were now quite oblivious to my presence, held taut within the rapture of sound. The dirge reached a climax of intensity, then breathed away to nothing. There was silence, the rustling of trees, a hiss from the fire. Then they all scrambled up, talking and bantering, and began to disperse. The girl took my arm. She looked captivating in the moonlight. She made me understand that I was welcome to stay the night in the camp, but I needed to get away.

The moon was by now bright enough for travelling. She led me through the woods, gliding along the faintest of tracks until we reached the open path, where she tiptoed up, brushed my cheek with her lips, and melted away. I waited a few minutes, then walked briskly back to the inn. I was anxious to get down on paper what I retained of the music. Evidently, I didn't.

I left for Salzburg, Paris and home.

I made several trips in subsequent years, amassing a stock of material that later formed the foundation of a promising academic career, and contributed not a little, I like to think, to the now-flourishing discipline of ethnomusicology.

I can review that career from here at my desk: two collections of folksongs (for which I can claim no credit); several books on methodology and field-studies; a score of monographs, a pile of lecture-notes. Not, after all, impressive as a legacy to posterity. I feel I have somehow failed to fulfil that promise, have been held back in some way—a view shared by my colleagues, I might add. My enthusiasm, my dedication, have been vitiated by—what? But take this article, for instance—in all probability, I will miss the deadline.

In fact, I am not at all sure, now, that I will even finish it.

Notes for an Abandoned Novel

Adopt a working title, to at least get going, get over the block. Anything.

Explosion in the Cathedral.
(Eliot. Carpentier [indefinite article] – slide from Revolutionary ideals to bloody actuality. Develop?)

*

Parallel cathedrals:
       (i) Universe. Existed prior to the Big Bang in the form of the Word. Translation into actual Being, Literality, a short-circuiting. Possible theme?
       (ii) Secular cathedrals: university, art gallery? Carpentier again – a fugitive seeking refuge in a concert hall during performance of Eroica. Could solve stuctural problem – use a man on the run as pseudo-plot, (Narrative nostalgia)
       Who? Bomber, victim, fall guy, betrayer? Any will do. It's just a device.

*

All too schematic.

*

Simulate the Big Bang – explosion in a printer's, words condensing into matter, a long congested paragraph gradually disentangling into thematic strands

*

Too ambitious, too experimental. Frighten the publishers. Write at random, see what happens.

*

a fresh sheet of paper   bleak white coolgrained   as he grasps the pencil his head lolls in a momentary lapse but he's focused now concentrated   tongue protruding   moving harmonically with the pencil point its first dot on the virgin white   a line jagged hesitant   now taking off vertically a smooth ascent into the upper right quadrant now a forty degree turn   describing a rhomboid   back down to a point level with the starting point   another downward vertical completes the structure he can start putting in the windows   next the oblong of the plaza   now the cross-hatching of the shadows and he can rest for a moment head rolling in the lapse of tension

adjusts the angle of the pencil point the strokes thick smudging for the doodle of the shrubs potted trees drift of tarmac beyond the plaza

another adjustment of angle to create the populace   pedestrians dog stalled taxi   bus   fill in the detail   signage street furniture fountain   A-board lovingly pointed   chased graffiti (the details he best likes)

tongue clamped in teeth he feverishly summons the surrounding blocks in an erection   undulating roofscape colonizing the white coagulating into a snaggled horizon   stray pigeon alighting on a distant pediment   swill of cloud

And it is finished.

head revolves with abandoned effort   grip unclenched finger by finger   the pencil falls he slumps in his chair   he scans the results to pronounce it good   but   something troubles some subliminal imperfection   he searches scans again   the angle of apex is wrong by two degrees three degrees beyond his tolerance

he breathes out holds up the paper   the tear runs silken down the
sheet rending tower taxi plaza fountainpool   beheading the dog
    he discards the halves   takes a white sheet of paper

☆

Develop idea of cityscape, the dead ends of Piranesi, desolate
colonnades of De Chirico. Introduce the fugitive. Make him the
bomber?

☆

'You attended the university?
'You were in the lecture room an hour before the blast?'
'I attended the lecture.'
'Was it that lecture that ignited your ambition?'
'A previous one.'
'And what was it about?'
'It was on Deconstruction.' (laughter in court)
'Have I understood aright? You attended a prior lecture on
the theories of one J. Derrida and they inspired you to plant a package
containing three dozen Blue Wizard A-Bomb fireworks in a cupboard
in the lecture room, timed to ignite after the later lecture? Were either
of these lectures pyrotechnical in character?'
'No, they were very dull.'
'You admit to planting the bomb?'
'I admit nothing.'

☆

Might be worked up. English Dept. linked to Dept. of Holocaust
Studies? (De-ironized rhetoric) Return to fugitive. No explicit identifi-
cation with bomber. A succession of fugitives, running through history?

he could feel the softened asphalt give way to paving beneath his heels and heard the dogs baying three blocks back so instinctively he kept straight on, resisting the obviousness of a doubling back into the dark where the dogs would anyway find him, and drawn to the light and safety if safety were possible of the paved plaza and nocturnal crowds. He had used even the reserves he hadn't known he possessed, even the dogs couldn't spur him on, but he calculated their baying as still three blocks behind which meant they hadn't been loosed were still on the leash and set himself to weighing up if that were a greater danger to be overtaken by dogs and handlers together, whether the men or the dogs were the more lethal for he was fading, his thighs swelling tightening but the square was round the next corner he could see the upward spillage of light though the pumping in his ears blocked the noise of the night-time crowd but he was here now and could lose himself until recovered and he stumbled as if shot into the huge deserted square.

The moonlight mixed with the streetlights regularly swagged along the crystalline grid to render spectral the distant moving train, though with the strobing of its carriage lights it could have been stationary. He had used railway tracks before, as wormholes, tunnels of darkness but this was on a walled embankment, the bricks in the hybrid light like ice, a glacis.

To gain time he began to weave in and out between the pillars of the vaulted colonnade, hoping the dogs as they followed his scent would entangle their leads but he knew it was a long shot so he zagged across the plaza picking at random from the radiating allées and instantly it was darker and he felt asphalt again. He panicked in case he had chosen his earlier path but then realized he couldn't have done for this path narrowed and after a right and left turn led to a dead end. //

Pine heavy on the air. Crashing through plaited trash and growth, denser as he struggles, a vegetal quicksand. Lostness, lost to time and light. At last a track, cutting through, a path to the clearing, a firebreak.

[Heidegger. Language wrenched into literality. Etymological interrogation.]

Woodsman's cottage.

Grim Tales. The red-hot dancing shoes. The Iron Stove – but the prince is not released; instead, the stove is lit. Gas.

*

Should be a novel in all this, but. Needs a strong ending. Shelve until

*

Parking strip on a light-industrial block. Suffused neon aura from the nearby high street. Late, but still well short of midnight. He is on his own, both street and home, out for air and take-away pizza.

The figure flared into view as he passed a 4×4, too sudden for aversion, breathing thickly – had he been running, or crouching, or was it rather nerves – and almost whispering, Please?

– Well?

– You have possible money, maybe mobile. I have need. We exchange.

– Over my dead body.

– If so.

The figure pulled a knife. It shone dully in the streetlight. He found himself sweating and suddenly angry. With the anger, an alertness. He decided to chance the old trick of looking past the man's head and suddenly grinning.

Reflexively he looked round, seeing nothing beyond his hood without turning his head. A kick to the groin, another to the ribs as he doubled over. He was down, scrambling to turn over and push himself up. He stamped on his wrist twice, kicked the knife away, picked it up.

Scared by the temptation, he dropped it through a drain grating. It still glinted, caught in the debris.

But the anger was still there, coursing through his bowels and prick. He kicked out again, to the chest, to the neck. Then he was hit by self-disgust or adrenalin overload, and buckled with nausea.

Finally he was able to straighten, sweat he assumed it was sweat trickling down his thighs, matting his hair, slowly able to walk away.

Haunted by that *able*, that ability to walk away.

For I never looked back, never checked. I don't know now if his neck was broken. I've heard nothing from the police.

GAVIN SELERIE

STAR-CROSSED

Cannon hump without fire

    barrel gaze (north)

        over
        east-west
        tunnel

a belt to enable
deeds
and shifts

              * * *

Walk through
to meet your name

    orange chalk or crayon
    furrowed
    with question mark

        cat-bird, red on blue,
        she who watches

mouth-curve
by lozenge cheek

※ ※ ※

Wee-zig-yik-keseyook (in old time)

   we are beneath
   an echo of sky

      the spirits' road

a hollow log,
stone canoe

※ ※ ※

This silence is to talk
paying out rope

     lives slipped

        you might
       recover

as a needle
crosses the circle

Maze of Crocodiles

What hope to accord   these two

     the vent and wall

that stretch forever

          one room above

          one beneath

great limestone columns and granite slabs

a twisting grid   dark to creep

as doors open to thunder

This niche is a little shop   or is it

     tomb-decked

a blind passage   baffling fret

of cordal resolve   you mock with brute tail

yelp to gasp

at what's not got

cased from desert dust and spew of lake

perhaps climb back   at tilt to sky

PADDOCK

Blank ingress
by a door that isn't there

                square spiral
        to place of last resort

            oblong citadel
            beneath
        concrete-gravel sandwich

and its sub-sub twin

                with engine room
        diesel-whiff

armour-bolted serpent

diver's mask gauges

distributor
spring-mattress
skeleton

rusty ducts
down whitewashed corridors

ceiling drip sticks,
fungal floor cones

message & telegraph hatches

vacant map grid
under northern heights

GPO packed up and gone

NICKY HAMLYN

PENUMBRA

Penumbra (2003) is a 16 mm black and white silent film, composed entirely of identical-ly framed shots of square, white bathroom tiles. Both camera strategy and shooting scheme were determined strictly by the formal properties of the subject—a square framed on three sides by a rectangle, and the white flat subject is all but indistinguish-able from the screen onto which its image will eventually be projected. The work is formed as a continuously evolving image, an effect that is achieved by dissolving the shots one into another, such that each new dissolve begins before the previous one has finished. (A dissolve is actually a fade-in superimposed on a fade-out, and the dissolves here were created 'in-camera', using a tool to wind the film backwards and start the next shot before the previous one has ended, as opposed to the usual industrial method, whereby the process is undertaken by laboratory technicians when the film is finally printed from edited camera rolls).

The dissolves do not function in conventional film-grammar terms as transitions from one shot to the next. Rather, the dissolves *are* the film: it is the resulting process of con-tinuous mutation of an image that retains certain constant features—mainly the vertical division between two adjacent tiles—that is the film's 'subject'. In this sense dissolves are used in an opposite way to the norm and thus the film may be seen in part as a reversal of one mainstream cinematic hierarchy, that between shots and cuts (excluded from this is, among others, Dziga Vertov, for whom the kinetic event occasioned by the cut was the defining feature of movie film). Making the dissolve the effective subject of the film emphasizes what is true of all films, that they exist as an image in flux, that usually we look past this truth to the representations unfolding in the pro-filmic space.

Movement occurs through mutations in the image as opposed to camera pans or tilts or staged action, such as the movements of actors. In practice these mutations are cre-ated through the way the dissolves bring in shadows, and occasionally objects, which impinge on the uniform grid. Informing this idea of movement through mutation are historical examples, such as the forty-five minute zoom in Michael Snow's film *Wave-length* (1967) or certain sections of Wilhelm and Birgit Hein's methodical study of filmic pseudo-movement, *Structural Studies* (1974). In these examples, movement is the optical —'virtual' in contemporary terminology—effect of the sliding of zoom lens elements to magnify an image, or of the image being defocussed. In the latter case, what actually happens in the de-focusing process is that the graphical disposition of shades of grey shifts on the screen as we watch, even if this is actually experienced as a loss of focus.

Penumbra's spatio-temporal grid structure parallels the structure of the film-strip, which is similarly grid-like: spatial in its actual physical form, spatio-temporal in its manner of operation.[1] In this sense the work is medium-specific, since video images, by contrast, are presented not as a rapid sequence of discrete frames, but as an electronic signal composed of a rectangle of horizontal lines of variable luminosity and colour, which are continuously refreshed by an electronic 'flying spot' that scans the image from top to bottom, left to right. In modern flat screens the pixels are always 'on', and are stimulated by voltages that cause them to glow momentarily.

The issue of medium specificity here is raised in a manner that attempts to avoid a concomitant commitment to essentialist characterizations, i.e. the reduction of a medium to its supposedly essential constituents. But where a work's concepts and/or structures address, and are informed by, unique features of a given medium, it is legitimate to talk about medium specificity. Thus *Penumbra* draws certain parallels between its own form and the technological characteristics of its medium, which would be illegitimate if applied to video.

Accusations of reductiveness have often been made by critics whose analysis is itself reductive or in some sense prescriptive and thereby essentialist, albeit in a different way. In a famous polemical essay on the problems of experimental/artists' film, 'The Two Avant-Gardes', Peter Wollen, states: 'The frontier reached by this avant-garde (the "experimental" (artistic) as opposed to the poly-semic cinema of Jean-Luc Godard and others) has been an ever-narrowing preoccupation with pure film, with film "about" film, a dissolution of signification into object-hood or tautology'. 'Cinema', Wollen argues, 'is a multiple system'.[1] What Wollen has done here is to identify the alleged abandonment of signification as an innately reductive move. His assertion is based on the proposal that 'Cinema is a multiple system'. Yet even such self-referentially titled films as George Landow's notorious 1966 work *Film in Which There Appear Edge Lettering, Sprocket Holes, Dust Particles, Etc.*, are always 'about', or have inscribed in their material forms, many things; light-play, kinesis, rhythm, time and its experience as duration, and, so long as a camera is used, indexical processes, representation and reference: 'Film, "motion picture" and "still" film, unlike painting and sculpture, can achieve an autonomous presence without negating iconic reference because the phenomenology of the system includes "recording" as a physical fact'.[2] In other words, all films made with a camera wrestle with questions of representation, even if the film's subject is only a sequence of differently coloured, lightly textured surfaces, as in Sharits' *Ray Gun Virus* (1966), which is composed entirely of blank coloured frames, or indeed, *Penumbra*, whose frame is mostly filled with the white surfaces of bathroom tiles. The second of Wollen's assertions, on which the first is premised, is covertly prescriptive, since it implies that because Cinema is, normatively, a multiply audio-visual system, this is what films should be or should aim to be. In other words, in contrast to a film like *Penumbra*, films, Wollen urges, should deploy the full range of possible signifying systems; iconic images, text, soundtracks, representational images of landscapes, objects, actors, etc. But why should films be composed of these things, just because they can be and have been (Wollen's paradigm is Godard's 1967 film *Two or Three Things I Know About Her*)? If we abandon the assumption that essentialism entails reduction, Wollen's argument could itself be accused of being tantamount to essentialist, or at least prescriptive.

Penumbra aims to raise questions around the idea of what an image is, what film is and how a non-contingent relationship, i.e. a determinate relationship, can be established between the apparatus—camera etc—and subject matter. It is composed of moving representations, and thus offers an already complex experience, as do even the most minimal of films.

―――

[1] Wollen, Peter, 'The Two Avant-Gardes', in *Studio International* (London, November/December 1975), repr. in *The British Avant-Garde Film, 1926–1995*, ed. Michael O'Pray (University of Luton Press/Arts Council England, 1996), pp. 137, 141

[2] Paul Sharits, 'Words per Page', in *Film Culture*, 65–66 (New York, Anthology Film Archives, 1978), p. 31

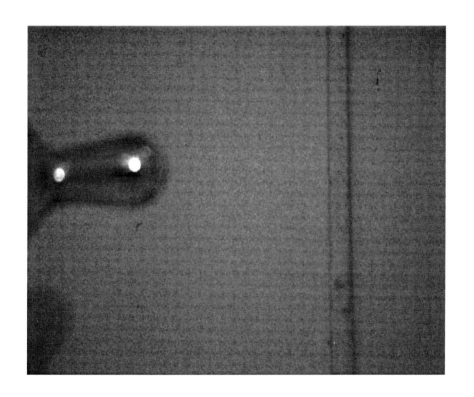

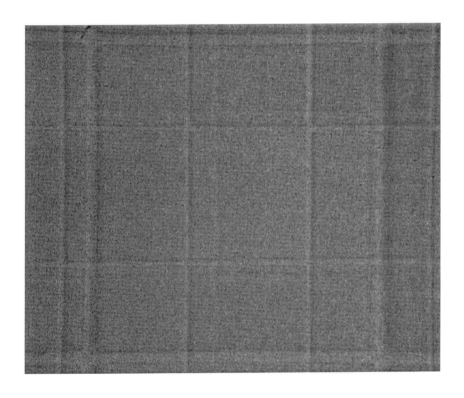

MICHAEL FARRELL

WILD PDFS

In a Pub

xxx the letter began, on the blank page, with poems attached
xx as if to reassure the recipient, or calm or stimulate them, or
x to sweeten separation. i said i was tired, i said i was blond, i
sat there watching my grandmother read poems to the crowd

[cut the glove]

they did not know they were near the end of the heyday of the
letter, that the next generations would find new ways to
organise and distribute their thoughts. i: i. mum: where's your
father got to? i: where've you got my father to? mum: hold
your lips in like a man, like a badly-reviewed man. my sister
sits in the chair by the bed, with an eye patch and a parrot to
match: some come from circus families, i don't. my father in
the hospital saying, this is not poetry, what i'm saying. my
brother with the camera saying tell me what to shoot. sunday
night, heavy machinery wars with rain. someone walks off the
field like they're tired of the game. i: library. i: lie down

[look at phone]

the bird flies around and around in the chimney like a ballet
dancer and we laugh at first. at first the bird seems so unusual
and sounds so funny with its song muffled by the chimney. but

after a while we understand that life in the chimney is a kind
of punished decadence. bird: i can't hear you, i can only hear
myself and memories of soot and the things it says, and bricks

[yearn]

bring in a professional. assemble again the pdfs and jpgs with
the eyes cropped, but lips that you'd recognise by tasting

[gesture to the tradition]

erase the names on the board. they had begun to appear like
words-as-saints. the animals without legs, and the animals
with many legs. the former pinning the latter. the microphone
has no affect of its own, yet draws us to say all kinds of things

[plates wobble]

i: your bad. you: behind you. other: we can manage. other:
a new mode that will make everyone want to copy you. i walk
towards the embankment with receipts in my pocket, fading

[open car door]

XING

On a Road on a Screen

three women lived at the palatial grotto apartments
at the crossing. people would go to them for advice
one was optimistic, one was pessimistic, the third
ambiguous. which one you got you couldn't
predict. someone i know went to complain about
the president, for destroying libraries, laws, the
peace. the woman asked, is the president more like
a frog or a cardboard box? two girls disappeared

[like glass]

they were not smart, pretty or liked. the principal
described them as 'a couple of dickweeds'. my
wife agreed that society was hell and encouraged
my railing. she sneered at those that went off to
work each day. 'providers' she called them. there
will always be threats to your marriage. if you
poison them a little each time they come round
they'll eventually get rooted inside. floating out to
sea. getting clean, letting all the guilt rise to my
epidermis. chopping wood and sending it off in
packages to the salvation army. making pies for the
bishop and the chief of police and the crime bosses

[you are a caterpillar]

using pink icing so every wedge is a pink triangle

going down their aching throats. taking nineteenth
century classics and making them medieval so they
can be understood. he's a jackal in the sack they
say; she loves to breathe. between or through
fences, almost anyone can get. he's a wombat in the
hay, a real alligator on legs, a two-donkey
balancing act. a little bit of syntax goes a long way

[what's the price?]

[cual es el precio?]

parked at the crossing, the ship of scholars waits

[something shimmers around a corner]

WHAT I'M DOING IN MY STUDIO

Going over

there are vehicles passing by and i record them
when i'm trying to record something else. a
history of bats flying in front of the moon, lying
by a rock in the dark, putting a swan's feather into
a cup of hemlock, or feeling shall we say. it is all
between letters, between thoughts of elevation and
the fruit of tears. i go over a rail: i'm always going
saying, someone's sick, alone, dying who needs me

[the glow of fire]

when you write, when you live in the room where you write
and naturally the line becomes your own, of wheat and posts
of queues of aggrieved and sore-footed people. there are more
i'm forgetting i'm sure. those on ships, trying to get a handle
on the romances they've read and those they've been told and
how little they resemble their own. they tell the children to
start every story with a fly, an honest fly. but the children run
from the flies and down to the beach or into the swamp. we
are sheep, they say. we're accounting everything you take
from our backs, and the doctor comes and removes their
skin birds and charges them sixty dollars per. while i am trying
to run my office and drive my car, and keep those who need it
in hand, and am called a lieutenant for it, with the irony of
foot soldiers, that write such wringing, unreadable verse. a
slice of lightning comes to the page, and presents the monaro
in frost and snow. each dog is lined up in half an old tank or
drum or crate for something once. a crow count the barks like
a calculator. they are sitting in the sunroom, no someone is
typing up each cattle bell, each track that comments on the
grass. then another walks towards them and says there's no
word for that in russian, yet there is a painting. this is all
decades ago, when the previous self-consciousness was
invented. when they would go to the gate as i go to my door
and bang music on their own leg if they didn't want to break
the jar of honey with joie de vivre and eat an oyster they'd
dived for themselves—or their mother had—that morning

[a monday]

KELVIN CORCORAN

from

FACING WEST

We hang suspended above the city,
jigsaw pieces thrown into the air;
the islands and the sea, the Penticlean hills,
the Parthenon and Syntagma Square unconstituted,
flicker and fall in bright array as time stops.

Those relationships of men and women turn over and over,
collapse into Saronic blue, the arms of the darkening coast
under the flood of stars over the Argolid and Arcadia;
falling and falling we fear nothing, only the end of thought,
to be layered in dust, seeing Phidias and the face of Athena.

Lydian luxury: the invention of coinage
sent seismic ripples pelagic,
electrum wrinkling the face of the Aegean
made the whole world a subduction zone.

Lydia on the caravan routes of the east,
flooding the Maiandros and Hermos Valleys,
whispered, *man is money* in Smryna,
ships head west on the old conditions dissolved

Unload debt slavery and economic facts,
the propensity for genocide on the borders,
a handsome stranger at the door ready to trade,
commodities rise and fall singing their own song.

Look what I've got, said Croesus, hands blazing,
my treasure house, my flashy power,
my lion and bull imprinted on your palm;
the abstract weight fits, shaping all you hold.

Eleanor at the tavern that night saying
—Of course the government has a plan B,
we run this business, even we have a plan B,
you see, they have a plan what to do, if if if.

People are tir/ed, years the money going,
how long now is this, not knowing what?
So now €200 is a lot, it was 500, but is a lot,
a lot more than nothing, people are tir/ed.

Plan B: dog poets of the Mani bark your lot,
send up your poem of despair unmeasured,
slung into the dome of night your distress flares
fall to the ground burning and you bark bark.

There are crossing points and they belong to Artemis;
any journey is an accumulation of crossing points.

They are marked by shrines, hidden tunnels and entrances,
the trash of sacrifice embedded in the mass of fibrous roots.

From Argolid to Arcadia, from Messinia to the end of the land
we drive the empty post-crash roads of ruined commerce.

Through the deep catalogue of our dealings and mineral certainty,
Artemis, torch bearer, depicts the lot of us moving off.

The journey is never personal—and is always personal,
a hole tapped in the skull, a child curled by her mother.

Our actions autonomous, joined, as if by thermal imagery,
the heat conveys red purple red our dance on hollow ground.

The road takes a final turn to Matapan and the double sea,
enters the inhabited darkness dressed in beads of light.

Above the sparkling sea displayed
on the stone steps rising to the chapel
permanent black marker boxed in white
—FILIA KOK SUSTS—

From here the Messenian gulf receives
the meeting of the Aegean and middle sea;
a short way out the water is 4 miles deep,
unnamed bioluminescent forms thrive.

Under darkness village dogs bark in Greek,
dog counterpoint shreds the starry sky;
the waves turn and turn about, barely tidal,
barely tidal the stain on the harbour wall.

Two old men talk dressed in fawn skins,
holding wands, ivy crowns their heads;
—But the very thought of dancing, cut and caper
makes me falter, it's not for me.

—Come on, let's get on with it, just a few steps,
up the mountain and show respect.
We think them old and foolish, twittering,
then the bloody fool enters and takes charge.

Up there on Cithaeron rivers run, women run
without memory and smiling confinement,
pines waver, animals feed, that song sounding;
come on, step up, show respect.

Ino took on her dead sister's baby, she had no choice,
the one unharmed by the thunderbolt that orphaned him.

Keep him safe, urged Hermes, as he landed out of the blue,
—You'll inherit the sea, the story of your sisters, Ino of the waters.

She kept him indoors, unseen by sun or moon,
those drones of spiteful gods plotting smoky vectors.

Dionysus, bright light, you beacon face darling, she sang;
the boy never slept, full of leaping life and hard to hide.

Later, driven to streaking madness by Hera, Ino ran,
her own son, tortured Melicestes, wrapped in her arms.

Under a spinning sky she saved him from her husband,
and mocked by her sister, hurtled the air into whiteness.

She curled her toes over the bite of volcanic rock,
took her dive and entered the deep as Leucothia.

Meanwhile Dionysus lounged in the fields of Lydia,
blossomed and swam in the rolling golden river.

Cushioned by roses and lilies on the dewy banks,
he auditioned his party friends for orgy and riot.

—Hang around, blow a flute, flick a drum, he said.
—Oh she's nice, he said, and the celebrity circus moved on.

Before, Ino had a hand in the dismemberment of Pentheus,
grasped and tore and danced the scatter dance in the meadow.

Inos meaning sinew, erotic prompt, the many versions manifest
but none of this is reliable, just dubious etymology, speculation.

As Leucothia she ran atop the white waves and found her name;
her life was in the sea, diving to save the drowned.

Under a spinning sky she hurtled pliant into whiteness,
ready for the dive, Ino of the waters, Leucothia of the deep.

She would listen to country music driving home,
decisions made, hands steady, tuning in and out;
certain colours worked for her on the windscreen,
the headlights reaching forward into the future.

White—meaning blue of the familiar hills,
darkness rushes by like a bow wave forgotten;
from a capsule of dials and calibrated thought
she splashes home to open her mouth and speak.

I heard this song on the radio, I just
I thought it was but no, I don't know,
it filled my head, I just wanted to be here,
the road a lyric, like the wings of song.

I saw an island on the mainland
trees by the waves, the south breathing
from Lebanon on Tyrian seas.

I saw the king of the wet drive his car
over soundless calm and the city of Cadmus
it looked like starry sex or Memphis.

He entered the women's apartments
sought the unguarded chamber of Europa,
she was long-gone ferried to the west.

Fountains spouted and fell unattended
desire sprinkled over the earth
and Dionysus sang a hymn to himself.

The party over, why was he there at all?
There was a girl and he was lovesick,
the cestus cinched around his sticky heart.

Comeuppance had him saying anything
just to have her in the springy woods,
reproaching the sky and darling cedars.

I will give you Bacchants for your bridechamber
and satyrs for your chamberlains,
I will make my mind a parade dancing in the street.

Girl, you have the blood of Cypris,
I will I will—all the old jibber jabber,
rejected he left with a thought of Ariadne.

He quit Asia for the cities of Europe,
to rattle the palace of Pentheus
and ready another scatter dance.

From the garden we see the stars turning
and we're sure that these words won't fly;
I was thinking rather of the silver birch
sweet and limby reaching out in the night.

There it shows green again, green sparks,
I was thinking rather of you, your face
staring up steadily in the lit doorway
and the taste of you filling my mouth.

No man looks at me like you, you really look;
and there goes the song running for the exit,
the mystery dance slides us across the floor
flips the order of things in the inhabited world.

I see you with my hands, the colour of your stare
in dark rooms, eyes open, stroke by stroke aswim,
a night spent turning the day inside out,
late late writing the book of wonders.

Indeed Dionysus seems always on tour, rolling into town,
India, Thrace, Thebes, Crete, various islands, like a rumour;
leaving a trail of dead women discarded, as if in a ballad,
Dionysus with his village song and clodhoppers ascendant.

Dionysus is always arriving somewhere, hennaed, pissed,
his mouth in our mouths—sings, let the vines grow over me;
surrender, whether you surrender or no, the oyster his world,
what's not in his hands, made-up, comforting gibberish.

Dionysus, standing there, says—water won't slake it,
his middle dynamic like background hum ineluctable;
Lydia, Phrygia, Persia, Bactria and Arabia claim him
launched from the Asian seaboard like a prick torpedo.

IAN BRINTON

My Mother's Painting

It seems, upon occasion, that the past can seek us out. A shark's fin slicing through water might be perceived from some distance above and its determined action, sensing and tracking down its quarry through the waves and over the years, might be observed by the steady analyst of movement.

On June 7, 2015 my wife and I were visiting friends in Lavenham, a wealthy and attractive medieval village in mid-Suffolk. We had been invited to lunch with Richard and Jo. It was a Sunday and having arrived rather too early as a precaution against turning up late we parked the car near the High Street and decided to have a look round. As was advertised on walls and gates around this well-preserved collection of half-timbered houses it was Open Gardens day, an annual event during which visitors were invited in to gaze at hollyhocked borders with their Downton touches. Kay and I walked gently around the town stopping now and then to peer in at various shops advertising local produce: honey, jams, and slices on porcelain cake stands. One attractively substantial eighteenth-century house had thrown open its gates announcing that there was a garage sale taking place on the gravel within. This was no car-boot sale but an altogether more rarefied presentation of things brought down from attics or up from cellars. As we sauntered in, my eyes glanced downwards at a watercolour painting propped up against a well-turned table-leg. It was a framed picture of anemones. Stopping in my tracks I turned to Kay and said "My mother painted that." Kay had seen one of my mother's watercolours before. I only had one and it was hanging on the wall at home. "Yes," she said, "your mother painted that." I must point out here that my mother was killed in a car accident forty-seven years ago when our family was living in Keston near Bromley in North Kent. I had been in the car at the time but was fortunate to escape with minor scratches.

I stood just staring at this painting.

The rather composed lady who was sitting in a garden chair nearby and who was obviously the seller of the picture announced: "It's a real painting, you know. A real watercolour painting."

"I know. My mother painted it."

Looking somewhat bemused the woman explained that she had had it for nearly fifty years and that her mother had bought it in some jumble sale down in Kent near Biggin Hill. "I'm afraid that that's a long, long, way away from here!"

"I know. We used to live two miles away from there."

I explained that my mother had died in 1968 whilst we were living near Biggin Hill and that my father must have thrown the painting out along with all my mother's belongings since he and I were set to move house a few days after she was killed. It was only at this point that I realised that since we had moved house, my father and myself, I had never again seen any of my mother's private belongings. It's just that I had never thought about it until now. Her life had simply gone. She was dead and therefore she didn't move house with us.

The lady sold me the painting for £10 and went on to explain that her mother was also now dead. She had moved to a town further along the North Kent coast and had died there.

"I don't suppose you know it, it's so far away. It's called Faversham."

"Kay and I live in Faversham," I said.

"Good Heavens!" she said. "Well, she was a Catholic and she is buried in the graveyard there, by the Catholic church."

"Tanner Street," I said and the lady's eyes looked a little scared.

I explained that we lived about two hundred yards from that Catholic church. And that my mother's name was also Kay.

Nobody can read someone else's mind. All we can see is that shark's fin of expression slicing through the space between us. It warns us of the body of thought just out of sight. Lunch was eaten, the day receded and anemones hang upon the wall at home.

ROBERT WALSER

translated from the German by

WILL STONE

Summer Night

It was night. A young man was sat in his room beside a lamp reading *Faust*, but as he read, he was asking himself from time to time if he should continue his reading or go down into the street. It was so lovely outside, the moon so bright. Next to the young man lay a sheet of paper. This paper seemed to be the draft of a letter: perhaps one of those letters that you write ardently until the moment when you are distracted halfway through by all sorts of strange scruples. The young man rose from the table and approached the open window through which a breath of night entered the great illuminated room, like an amiable peaceful thought. Already at that hour he had heard while reading the footsteps of numerous passers-by. During his reading he sensed himself down there among the strollers going to and fro so peacefully. Now he was looking out the high window, perched up there above the street as if suspended in mid air, the serene nocturnal image which shifted along the length and breadth of the silent square, and he smiled at the isolation of his attic window lit by the moon, of his nourishing solitude, which to him seemed as beautiful or perhaps even more beautiful than all the rest. Naturally he would happily have closely followed a pretty woman at once distinguished and alluring, Mlle L, for example, to admire her silhouette and her graceful movements. He would willingly have joined the customary evening promenade, following in the footsteps of other strollers, but he felt himself at least as contented, if not far more contented where he was and that is why he remained at his window. 'Oh wonderful night' he told himself in a low voice, 'How lovely you are, and you divine moon, how lovely you are.' From the café garden situated just beneath the young man's window, a concert of flute and violin with its sweet phrases, its joyful tears, its nostalgic exuberance, its stifled sobs, its peals of laughter and its lament like the blackbird's song carried this musical banter, like a swaying game, a mirroring of life that rose to his attentive ear. The young man adored those sounds and became drunk on them. Little by little, down below, the street became silent. The occupant of the room extinguished the lamp. He desired nothing more around him than the gentle light of the moon.

Morning Hour

In that moment just before waking, I had a strange dream of great beauty, which half an hour later I could no longer recall. After rising, it re-entered my consciousness. I saw a lovely woman and brimming with juvenile exuberance I worshipped her. I felt myself marvellously composed and exalted by the radiant youthfulness of my beautiful dream. I dressed quickly. It was still dark. A breath of wintry air brushed me lightly through the open window. The colours were so sharp, so unforgiving. A cold and noble green struggled with an emerging blue; the sky was filled with clouds of a vivacious pink. The awakening day, that still wore the moon's necklace like a silvery jewel, seemed to me of a sacred beauty. Silent, joyful and intoxicated by the beauty of the dream and the grace of the day, I hurried to go out, into the air, the street. Seized by the will and a young man's hope, I had gained a boundless and gentle confidence in myself. I no longer wished, genuinely no longer wished to think of anything at all, nor wished to explore what had left me so serene. I gambolled across the mountainside and I was happy. How strong you feel when at peace, how that renewed confidence makes you joyful and how good it feels when the head and the heart swarm with fresh hopes.

———

Sommernacht, Morgenstunde in
Robert Walser, *Prosa aus der Bieler Zeit, 1913–1920*
Sämtliche Werke in Einzelausgaben, herausgegeben von
Jochen Greven (Frankfurt am Main, Suhrkamp, 1985)
Will Stone translations are from forthcoming Prosa
twenty-eight short Walser pieces, most of which
have not previously appeared in English

D S MARRIOTT

POUNDLAND

The austere margin, from highrise to taxi
whoever enters here will see hope
rising from envy, their seasons opening amid branches,
where we feast our obese flesh on tiers
of cost-priced plenty, the newly-owed duly begun,
counting the junk as though the whole thing, in the end,
could be accounted for, yet never enough for benefit's benefit.
From c-aisle to counter, hauling shamelessly
whoever comes here knows the price
of exultation, the shores submerged in dross
where everything is changed to wager, and food and rent
are discovered to be counterfeit, floating free on a gigantic ocean—
like boats listing, taking in too much, voyaging out because empty.
Alas, the illusion wanes quickly,
the northern tides are mere glass, the waters hold no vision:
a seagull flies across the bows of the familiar,
salt-stained by sewage; and when the arrow is loosed
there is neither loss, nor modesty.
Why are we so enslaved to these enchantments?
God knows it's not worth saving yerself for.
Saved enough to ruin yerself didn't yer,
when your own proper store is counted unearned . . .
Its the last rule of the undeserving.
This is what we take from the temple: the gleam of first things,
a cynicism discounted for want of the unwanted,
the sums uncountable yet countless, a windfall
only some can ill afford, needing no credit.

So down the aisles we went,
beyond the tills, the tiers clogged with indigence,
the clarity of the rules like sentences,
here, where desire leads happiness always follows,
and to be without is to be alone and desperate.
Go on then. Chuck us those empty tins.
Hurry up. Stop stopping behind.
If you lose one the whole world is ours.
But who's to say how much is nothing, when naught is all,
and the expense is worth less, however brief the forfeit,
than the yearning—here, where the price
is, more often than not, unearned—and what remains
is the sum of our famishing, the bye taken away from us?
The day's promise burns bright with the vicissitudes of longing.
The most lasting delusion is never the thing that lasts,
but that which comes and says believe, learn to resemble
the endless avatars of our enduring.
For the citizens of tomorrow, we will be like sirens,
doling out songs for the untraveled distances,
the waters, where they enter it, neither a lure nor a symbol.
Come on then. We're all one pound owing.
Damned because the buoys and tugs are scherzos.
And the drays: duettos.
Even the deliveries are tremulating with impatience!
So its five down with a pony on top fer interest—it's a steal
for whose who know their pomegranates from their oranges,
just sums from the desolate moorings
never ours to arrive at, or own.
Look at em. So envious, grasping their boxes like unmuzzled dogs.
The further they get in the dirtier they become, and when yer
walk down the aisles you can smell the filth:
the desires that fostered them, raised to the level of existence,
beside the sins they covet, irreparably impoverished, and skint.

MANDY PANNETT

NAMELESS

1

I should give the narrator a name. Not that she has one in the poem, nor in the title some Victorian scholar chose: *Wulf* and *Eadwacer*—an off-putting mouthful with no mention of the woman who wants to tell her tale.

Only nineteen lines of text—less in the original so carefully scribed and tucked into the Exeter Book. Yet these lines provide more puzzles than any bard's song in the mead-hall or Saxon riddler's guessing game. Reams of paper have been used on argument and counter-theory, single words sliced to the root with bitter refutations. If all this was written on skin, how many calves would lie dead?

Yet, in this barren but beautiful scene, anyone may interpret the air.

2

Torrents of rain match her mood. She sits on a hillock of cold, wet grass, buries her face in her hands and sobs. She is wild with love but there is no hope, for her lover is hunted by the law and only her thoughts can follow. Can she save him, clear his name, dodge the brute who would force her to the ground in rape? Bouts of sickness suggest a child. *Wulf, min Wulf,* she cries. He will not return. She is the heroine of her own Soap, at the mercy of every twist.

3

These are waterlogged days. No Dutch engineer has yet drawn up plans, no civil-war prisoners, homesick and shivering, have been sent to the Fens to dredge and reclaim. There are islands here—places whose name-endings bring in the smell of salt and eels, marsh and bracken, shallow-green pools. Ely, Whittlesea, Welney, Stuntnea . . . here live men who walk stilt-high in fear of the swamps, push small fishing boats into the reeds, hurry through the darkness of woods where bandits hide.

Wulf is on one island, his girl on another. No wonder she weeps.

4

My thoughts are teased by an image of wool. Was she a peace-weaver, this woman, sent reluctantly in marriage to end a blood-feud, to reconcile enemies who plotted revenge in a Germanic version of West Side Story? The text seems too feral and violent for this. Threads in the story rip apart. *One may easily slit that which was never seamed*, says one translator, following the metaphor of cloth.

This could be the landscape of Philomela, who, violated and tongue-less, wove her tale of abuse and agony into a picture that others might read. This could be Arachne's web—a web without words but spinning with truth. Is there more than an elegy here? Is this a tapestry of blood where every stitch is pain?

5

Eadwacer: now here's a name to conjure with—property watcher, heavenly priest, woman's jailer/rapist/lover—or none of these; not a person
at all. Text is so easy to tamper with: a comma alters emphasis, a taller
initial turns a common to a proper noun.

You have done well, Eadwacer. Mentioned four lines from the end, and
then but once, and yet you've pushed and shoved your way into the title
(where the author needed none), made yourself co-star with Wulf, whoever he is.

6

Sacrifice and bloody gifts silt the ditches of these lines. Who called this
an elegy, a tale of love and loss? I think the poem reeks of guts, ripped
by fangs and teeth.

And overlaying shit and terror are the Saxon Beasts of Battle—Eagle,
Wolf, ferocious Boar—who scour the fields for bone.

7

'No!' screams a scholar in my ear. 'You hunt for narrative as if your life
depends on a linear shape. This is a riddle, trust me, longer than the
ninety others in the Book at Exeter, but just as much a kenning as the
ones that answer *Storm or Sword* or *Ice Inside a Water Butt*. Who knows, it's
doubtful, but it might be a quiz to trick a scurrilous mind that thinks the
answer must be *Penis* till a shout of sudden laughter cries *'It's Onion, fool!'*

8

That went past, this may too.

Do *Wulf's* nineteen lines belong elsewhere—an extract from the poem *Deor*? Is *Wulf* a missing section of that lament about a sad minstrel who lost his role and high position, and so became a wanderer, one who must endure his grief until the very end.

That went past, he says in refrain.

It is different for us, says the lover of Wulf.

9

Fen-surrounded islands—floating worlds of isolation. Here in marsh and forest were holes where refugees could hide—if they could endure the pain of arthritis from the constant damp, survive marsh fever and malaria in the heat-wave swamps.

Was Wulf an outlaw in these fens, subject to the common-law's pronouncement: *Caput gerat lupinum (May he bear a wolfish head)?* Such a victim could be run through with a sword, bound by vigilantes, held down in a village pond until he died. Many think the name of Wulf provides a clue as to his fate, see him crouched in Ely reeds like Hereward on the run. But surely he'd have offered money, paid a weregild to the injured, cleared his reputation of offence? Wealth could delete the most abhorrent crime.

A perfect setting for the sinner then, flatlands with cover under a vast grey sky. Ideal, as well, for the missionary-saints whose obsessive visions reduced them to skin and bone. We hear of Guthlac who, fistful by fistful, dug into the earth of a plundered barrow to make himself an oratory and cell. Here he lived, more than half-starved on his daily scrap of barley bread and cup of muddy water, fierce in his mission but terrified by howling winds and sounds of demons in the night—probably the voices of bitterns, cranes and kites, but to him they were fiends from hell.

The Fens are still full of ghosts, even though they have been urbanised, their waters taken from them. I remember a night at Welney—November frost and thick, thick fog. From the sanctuary across the fields the cries of wild geese filled the air, heart-broken spirits, it seemed to me, like those battlefield captives doomed to toil in the Fens in their garments of wet white wool.

It is said that Guthrac, on his deathbed, conversed with angels as scents of ambrosia filled his cell. Some compensation then, as St Audrey found. (A determined virgin in spite of two husbands, she founded the double-monastery at Ely where the Cathedral stands). Convinced that the tumour on her neck was a punishment imposed on her for wearing a necklace in her youth, she was promised, so documents say, that her body would shine and be incorruptible forever after her death.

'What is it . . . that you have let pass such a long time, that you have delayed to come? Why do you not want to remember that I am alone on this earth?'

So begins a letter written in the eighth century by a woman called Bert-gyth.

It continues:

How can you afflict the mind of me, who am naught, with constant grief, weeping and sorrow, day and night, through the absence of your love?

Such a letter might be written by any woman to a tardy lover, a dilatory husband, an unpunctual boy friend. Such a letter might be written by the woman in the poem to Wulf.

In fact Bertgyth, a nun, is writing from Thuringia in Germany to her brother in England. *No other brother will visit me, she says, or any other kinsman will come to me . . . oh brother, oh my brother, how can you afflict the mind of me.*

There are several letters, in similar tone, written by women to their brothers. Bonds of kinship were important to the Anglo-Saxons and especially so in times of long separation. Themes of loneliness are strong in the writings of nuns and female scholars who were frequently sent, often against their will, into convents or to communities abroad.

There is both sorrow and anger in the letters that survive—as there is in *Wulf* and *Eadwacer*. Could Wulf be the woman's brother? There are many who go with this interpretation and think the 'islands' are monasteries and that the poet-scribe used the act of writing to spill the word-hoard, express a deep emotion.

12

'Not true', mutters a voice. 'Far-fetched, crazy talk. *Wulf* and *Eadwacer* is a charm, a charm against tumours or wens as they called it. Look at the language of invocation, the refrains, the narrative . . .'

'Rubbish', cries another, 'it's a metaphor for the Christian Church in its fight against the pagan world. Two islands represent the clash, the differences . . .'

'You pluck fantasies from air', insists a voice of logic. 'The poem is obviously incomplete, parts are missing that would make sense. Look at the damage to the Exeter Book—pages torn out, knife marks all over it, beer stains in several parts . . .'

'No, it is complete'. This from the voice of certainty. We are not the audience the poem was intended for. There must be a famous tale behind all this—an old Norse legend perhaps—and an Anglo-Saxon listener would know it well.'

'I have a better theory', cries a graduate, keen to make his mark. 'None of the things you say are true. There are children in this poem! Wulf is the woman's elder son, he is in danger and so is her infant, so is the whelp . . .'

13

Ah. The whelp. The biggest puzzle of all. *Our whelp*, says the text in translation, *will be carried by a wolf into the woods*. Whose cub? One from a pack of Fenland wolves? A love-child, offspring of Wulf? Of Eadwacer? A baby conceived in love or lust, marriage or rape? Theories mutter of unwanted children exposed to the elements, left to perish.

On this, the door-leaves of the mouth are sealed.

14

Where are they now? An insistent Anglo-Saxon motif. There are earth-steppers in this poem but their footfalls are light, point in several directions at once, lead only to bones in a peat bog that will never surface, never re-assemble.

And the author of this poem, who was she? Nun? Scribe? Story Teller? Or a woman who once told her tale to someone who liked it, sang it in a mead-hall or two so that others heard, added to it, altered some words, touched the poem with feather-light, finger-tip impressions of yearning and lament?

I saw a man standing, claims a riddle, a dead man walking who never lived.

How could this be?

As an image in water, comes the reply—and I wonder if this is a tiny clue to the mystery of *Wulf:* a reflection of light that flickers on a pool for an instant, even as it ripples into shadow and goes.

JOE LUNA

POEM

Woke up sad as rainbows, tailing the illegal Dropbox rally
from a standpoint of total inforescence in New Mexico, all doubt
undercover and surrounded with a bluish-pink demeanour

Your betting spreads, evidence without you goes at night
into the names of squealing fathers seeding paradigms, trussed
up in small remainders. Once I took cover there was nothing

Doing the elastic, as doe eyes settle into fasces, the gooey
dreamwork plagued millions for a chance to throttle the inevitable
enviable finale. It's justice in the language gamer, a series of

Delectable salts and proteins, rivals in the shadow of a basin. One
day last year we spoke, punching waste into oblivion
our gamma the entire cloud between our sim cards. Then as now

I motion to the ocean, bit by bit, soluble as ice-cream outside
the second embassy for networks bursting at the seams in loco
motive mesmerising pedalo. Collapse in foreign daylight only yours.

LOLA THOMAS

A Place in Time

G 8   FOSSIL MAN
Early Palæolithic Flint Implement, from Thames gravel, Maidenhead
About ½ natural size

BRITISH MUSEUM (NATURAL HISTORY)

FOSSIL FOREST, LULWORTH.

FRANCIS PONGE

translated from the French by

IAN BRINTON

from

FROTH AND BUBBLE

opening sections of
Francis Ponge, *Le Savon*, Gallimard, 1967
translated from the text established in
Francis Ponge, *Œuvres complètes, tome 2*
Bibliothèque de la Pléiade, Gallimard, 2002

I

The Address

Ladies and Gentlemen,

Perhaps you would care to listen . . . Well, at any rate you have already begun to hear . . .

BANG!

(Now did you hear that?) Because what you heard at that moment was the opening line of a literary text, . . . a public reading of a German text which had originally been written in French . . . That is, not written by me, the German announcer whose voice you are listening to, but by the French author whose words come to you from my lips.

Now, this is what he wrote.

Or, well, rather, if he were actually speaking, as he is of course through my mouth, he would *say, or, well actually he* does *say:*

This isn't what I wrote but, instead, it is what I am writing to you my German audience, for your ears.

I am in the process of composing the opening lines. I am no further ahead in the matter than you are; I'm not far off in front. We are going to move ahead, or rather we are moving ahead, together, with me doing the talking and you doing the listening. We are shoulder to shoulder in the same car. We are on board the same boat.

✻

However, truth to tell, where actually am I? I am sitting at my own table, in France, in my own house. Whereas you . . . God knows where you are! You know perfectly well where you are much more than I could possibly know. You also know whether or not you are really listening , as opposed to just hearing, whilst you go about your own business within the confines of your own apartment, perhaps even chatting away . . .

BOOM!!

From now on I am going to assume that you are listening to me. So . . .

LISTEN

✻

Ladies and Gentlemen,

When the suggestion was put forward that I should compose some literary text for your consumption a very interesting idea came into my mind of making good use of this occasion to bring to conclusion some writing, originally conceived a long time ago, which, despite many attempts, I have never managed to bring to completion.

With all due thanks both to you all here and to my own notion of us travelling along side by side, I intend to rectify this today in one way or another.

Thank you!

Picture me, in front of my desk, with the obligation of writing the text before me. On the left side of my desk there is a large file of papers containing my notes. An enormous file! Twenty-three years-worth of notes!

Now! Achtung! Attention! Attention please!

Listen carefully to the full weight of noise made by this large folder which I have just picked up, which I am lifting into the air, and with which I am going to deafen you by dropping back onto the desk.

WHOOF!

Did you hear that?

Right! Now I am going to open up this folder. But, before I do, let us look at the word inscribed upon its cover:

SOAP

Soap, Ladies and Gentlemen, die Seife, die Seifenkugel! Now you are fully aware of what this is! After all, you make use of it every day!

You will have a clear picture, shared by us all, of what is represented by this single word. It presents to us all one of the world's physical realities. And that, of course, includes me.

That said, for me personally, SOAP is, above all, centrally, today, this folder, this sacred collection of papers!

Ah, yes! Soap-file; paper-Soap. What aggravation over the past twenty or twenty-five years this SOAP has given me. With luck, however, today, within a few minutes I shall be washed clean of this burden! Come along, then! Let us open the file!

✿

First; let me give you good warning!

You are going to be rather surprised I suspect—on account of its not being a common feature of literary compositions—by the frequent but extremely precise repetitions to be found throughout the text. There will be occasions when you feel compelled to say "But the man is repeating himself! I already listened to this only a few moments ago". Well? Should I be offering apologies? Absolutely not! I am not very fond of apologising for myself and also, after all, these methods, as you will readily acknowledge, are central to the composition of music. Repetitions, reprises da capo, variations upon a theme, contrapuntal composition that you both allow for and appreciate in music; why should you shun them in a literary creation?

Can you answer that for me?

Well, now you have been advised!

That is the way I work and that is the way the birth of my ideas develop. And that is the way in which my mind moves forward. You want me to be honest don't you? You can't play tricks with the way inspiration flowers.

✿

Ladies and Gentlemen, here are the first notes that I scribbled down on paper in April 1942 at Roanne, a small town in the heart of France where my family and I were, as one might put it, in hiding as refugees.

This was in the middle of the war, a time of rationing, and soap, the genuine article, was in short supply. We were stuck with synthetic soap which didn't froth up at all.

It is possible that this is one of the subconscious reasons I had for giving the title SOAP to my germ of inspiration in April 1942.

Anyway, here are my original notes and, from now on, I shall not interrupt myself again.

No more commentary!

Just soap: SOAP!

II

SOAP

Roanne, April 1942

Soap foams and bubbles when I rub my hands with it . . .
The more it makes my hands smoothly smug and compliantly supple
        the more it froths in pearls . . .
Magic pebble!
Sculpted by air and water
it resolves itself more and more into clusters
of perfumed grapes . . .
overlapping, water, air and soap
glides into leap-frog, merges into new moulds
more physical than the result of a chemical interaction,
more like an acrobat, a gymnast . . .
Frothy rhetoric?

There is a lot to say on the subject of soap. It surrenders its own exact story; it exhausts its own subject down to its complete disappearance. This is the very object which beckons me.

✽

Soap has a lot to say for itself as it bubbles over with enthusiasm and garrulity. When it has concluded its speech . . . it has gone!

✽

A type of pebble, but not one that has been smoothly rounded by natural process, it slips through your fingers and melts before your eyes rather than lying there solid, to be washed by the waters.

The trick is to keep a hold of it in your fingers whilst rubbing it with an appropriately measured amount of water in order to extract from it a pearly froth of response.

If it is left in the water it just collapses in confusion.

✽

A type of pebble which, (*yes, that's it! a type of pebble-which*) does not permit itself to be fiddled about with by natural forces through whose fingers it slips and before whose eyes it melts.

Rather than let itself be rolled around in the water it gently vanishes from the eye.

✽

There is nothing remotely like it in the world of Nature. Assuming that you have succeeded in holding on to this object, whilst gently moulding it with the right amount of water, no pebble or puck or slippery stone will produce a similar reaction in your hand: a pearly slobber over-foaming with clusters of pompous bubbles.

Empty grapes. Soap-scented grapes.

Unmethodical clumps!

It gulps down the air and water spread over your fingers.

Although it can sleep inert and shapeless in a soap-dish it contains the power to compel our fingers to writhe in water making the green one bubble.

And so we slide from words themselves to slippery meanings with that dawning awareness of drunkenness, a frothing over, a shimmering, a cold explosion from which we can now withdraw our well-washed hands.

Soap may be a type of pebble but it isn't a natural one: it's alive, it responds and it's not simple.

It even possesses a sort of dignity.

It takes no pleasure from being rolled about by forces of nature and wouldn't waste its time with that; it is a slippery customer who will vanish rather than be rolled round in earth's diurnal course.

Compelled by the urgency of the time we were obliged to move from Roanne and I took my writing up again in Coligny, a village north of Lyon.

Nothing in nature is comparable to soap. There is no pebble as slippery in the hands—even if you do manage to keep a grip on it whilst rubbing it between the fingers—or one which exudes such a pearly froth in clusters of exuberant bubbles.

Shaped like empty-scented grapes, bubbles of soap gobble both water and air running through your fingers; they draw circles round the air and, without any great to-do, these lecherous, shimmering aquatic nymphs adopt a pulsing elastic form.

Enthusiastic, full-throated thereness.

Shimmering lucidity cold bubbling-over . . .

Yes. A shapeless shape, it squats in a saucer; it has the power to make our own hands softly servile and to abuse every drop of water; the power to make itself solicitous to our needs, to shift its shape so glibly as to dance with us non-stop in its robes and gowns and ballroom scarves. On our side we drain its energy down to the last drop . . . you may feel that there is something vicious in this interchange of mutual abuse.

(Nothing more resembles a kneading-trough than a wash-bowl but in a wash-bowl you'll find nothing but hands.)

. . . And so we smoothly glide from words to meanings . . . in a shimmering, lucid drunkenness, a bubbling-over, a cold frothing from which we emerge, and here's the rub, with hands which are more clean and more pure than they were when we started.

*

Soap was put together by man for the use of his body; however, it doesn't play along voluntarily. This still pebble is nearly as difficult to get a grasp on as a fish. There it goes, escaping to plunge back into the basin

like a frog . . . giving off, at its own expense, a puff of blue cloud to act
as a smoke-screen. . . .

☆

What a marvellous way of living is set before us by soap! Hardened
by the sun, its forehead clouds over and toughens up, wrinkles and crazes.
Although split by care it is only when unused and forgotten that it can
look after its own interests.

By contrast, when it basks, revolves and seems at its ease in water—it
becomes difficult to haul out—where it rolls around, agile and voluble—
it wears itself out with worrying speed and cannot live without paying
the price . . . Is this what we term the life of a dissolute . . . ? I can also
recognise here something of dignity . . .

☆

The principal virtue of soap is its voluble enthusiasm. It has the facil-
ity for self-expression. So simple, but it has never been said before. Even
by the advertising experts. And so! How much do *Piver* or *Cadum* offer
me?—Not a sou! It's never crossed their minds! However, we are going
to show them what we're made of . . .

☆

There is something to adore in the personality of soap. Why is it
adorable? Because it is supremely likeable and utterly individual.
Here you have a very ordinary pebble shape squatting flatly in the
most ordinary of saucers, often itself damaged, in the house.
Enter a man with dirty hands. And the overlooked soap exposes itself
to him. Not without a certain air of coquettishness. It gets itself up in

[128]

glistening veils of iridescence while at the same moment it seems to hide away, to vanish. None of nature's pebbles is as agile. And the trick now consists of keeping hold of it with your fingers and rubbing it with a sufficient amount of water in order to give rise to a pearly slobber whereas if it just remained submerged it would dwindle away in confusion.

Soap possesses a dignity all of its own. Although pebble-like it will not permit itself to be rolled around by the forces of the natural world. It slips between their fingers, sticks to the depths and dissolves before the eye rather than allow itself to be rifled by the surrounding waters.

Man abuses it. When he chafes it in his hands it bubbles over with jubilation. The more excited it gets, the more it slobbers and froths and the more supple, soft and pliant become his hands.

Magic pebble!

. . . The more air and water, the more it explodes with clusters of perfumed grapes.

Air, water and soap overlap each other, play at leap-frog, come together to form new items which are then blown apart by a puff, a smile, a little vaingloriousness, a slight exaggeration . . .

Or a heavy blast of water.

One may feel that I have overdone these metamorphoses, these variations; that my style has become a touch soapy, lathered, full of spume—like that which gathers around the nostrils of a horse in full gallop—.

It is intentional.

Knowing that a paragraph of reason or irony would be sufficient to brush clean, wash away and rinse everything out.

*(This version, titled "soft-soap-babble"
is from 3 June 43 at Coligny.)*

✳

There is nothing like soap in the rest of nature. No other pebble com-bines such magnificence with such modesty.

Truth to say, there is something very attractive about its personality. Its behaviour is unique.

It opens up with a cool sense of reserve.

It introduces itself with perfect self-control, with just a hint of scent. Then, when one comes to grips with it, I won't use the word fire of course, but what explosiveness! What exuberance in giving itself! What generosity! What unimaginable garrulity, almost unstoppable!

One may, of course, withdraw from the connection but the whole adventure in this brief affair—and here is the best part—leaves you with the cleanest pair of hands you have ever had.

✻

Because this object possesses so many qualities I am going to have to say a little more about it, to make it bubble before your eyes.

SOAP

Coligny, June 1943.

ABSTRACT

(Theme: intellectual ablutions)

If I wanted to show that purity is not achieved by silence but by some energy of language (under certain circumstances, a tiny laughable object held in the hand) followed by a sudden downpour of clean water,

What object springs more readily to mind than soap?

Urgent desire to wash hands.

Dear reader, I assume that sometimes you want to wash your hands?

For intellectual ablutions, reader, here is a text about soap.

✻

Coligny, June 1943.

. . . Here than, dear reader, to clean your mind (if you are one of my friends, you will feel an urgent need for this sometimes) here is a little sliver of *real soap*.

In truth, man cannot have a good scrub-up with just water, whether he is being drenched in a torrent, blown dry in perfumed breezes, nor with silence, nor with prayer (even if baptized to the waist in the river Jordan), nor with self-immolation in the darkest springs (despite all sorts of current views on that matter).

It needs—and this will do it, but it is essential—whether in the hand (or the mouth) something solid and less natural, something artificial and eloquent, something which expresses itself, develops and vanishes in the process. Something very much like language being used in certain circumstances . . .

. . . In a word: *a little bit of soap.*

✻

We need this kernel of azure clouds; this vortex of delicate spheres.

This prestidigitation, the prestige of a display behind which the memory dissolves.

The memory of all filth melts; but the worst solution to the whole matter would consist of your being led by either the prejudiced ideas of your parents or yourself into being ducked in some insipid tributary of the Dead Sea.

Skin like new! Brush up!

✻

[131]

Coligny, July 1943.

This egg, this flat-bottomed
dab—this little
almond, which
metamorphoses so quickly
(on the instant)
into a Chinese fish
With its veils and wide-
sleeved kimonos
Soap celebrates its wedding
with the water. Such are its wedding gowns.

✳

One never reaches the end
of soap!
    . . . However, it must be returned to its saucer, to its clear-edged being,
to its solemn ovality, its dry sense of patience and its restrained energy.

✳

Coligny, 6th July 1943.

ABSTRACT (withdrawn and dry in its saucer) AND DEVELOPMENTS
(pearly froth) of
SOAP (followed by a paragraph on rinsing with clean water).

For ablutions of the mind, a small piece of soap, well-handled, will
suffice. As opposed to a gush of clear water which cleans off nothing.
    Neither the silence, nor the suicide in the darkest springs, O uncom-
promising young man.

✳

Ah, yes! Nothing is to be achieved by taking up residence beneath the pump. Nor by basking in the waters of the Jordan. (A simple bowl would be more effective . . .) Unless one clutches (and makes use of) this seemingly ordinary pebble (with its magical properties) . . . and gives it the last word.

One hardly has to solicit it in order to achieve eloquence!

It releases such enthusiasm and shimmering chatter firstly into the hands of the one who releases it from its silence and then over the entire body of the liberator.

What a bubbling-over of which we must take note!

Perhaps you take my point and I could stop here. What! But the very nature of my subject permits me to enjoy myself and to ensure that you enjoy further slight but impressive developments of (as it were) an ephemeral and purifying kind.

*

Coligny, 8th July 1943.

SOAP

Thank God, a certain amount of babble is appropriate to the subject of soap or when soap is touched upon. Touching soap there is more babble than straightforward talk. And there is no point in worrying, in being anxious, about going over the same ground. One may, indeed must, blather. To blather is to say what? To become a little ridiculous, to make language a little ridiculous. Whilst always keeping a firm grip on the soap. Before placing it in its saucer and taking a break with a flush of pure water (a paragraph suffices for a turn of the tap).

And here is the marvellous bit: one comes out of this business with hands that are both more clean and more pure.

*

Now, let us go further and assert that for whatever cleansing process is contemplated, a piece of soap is central; let us say that that will do.

In fact, it is recognised that one cannot have a really thorough clean with just water. This would be the case even standing under cascades of the purest water. Or in the darkest and coldest depths of the spring's source where the temptation to commit suicide might overwhelm you, young man. Even if one were to plunge down into the well from which all truths rise. None of that would encourage the grime on the skin to bat an eyelid. Nothing is to be gained by living beneath the pump and risking hiccoughing one's life from birth to death. And I will only mention for the record the outdated solution of immersing oneself up to the waist, with arms crossed, in some minor tributary of the Dead Sea (water oozing into the Dead Sea) whilst touching with two wet fingers one's brow, navel and breasts in a swooping motion as if responding to a Papal Bull.

Give me an ounce of soap and a little bowl rather than that!

✻

There is much to be said on the subject of soap. Everything that it has to say for itself when one rubs it up in a certain manner with water. It seems also rather inclined to say a lot. Let it speak. Garrulous with enthusiasm. Until it fades away under its own theme. When it has finished bubbling over it is all gone. The longer it takes to express itself the longer its expression lasts; the more slowly it melts, the higher quality it is.

Needless to add, it always says the same thing. No matter to whom it speaks it invariably expresses itself in the same way.

Prattling pebble . . .

It is evidently clear that there is an almost limitless amount one might say about soap. Or might babble rather than say. A certain amount of gush is appropriate here. A certain keenness to let it all out.

May it not hesitate in always saying the same things and in the same way. And to speak in the same enthusiastic tongue to whomsoever. And the most marvellous result is that one emerges from this experience with very clean hands. That is the fundamental lesson.

And let it be also understood that the lesson is the very best for intellectual hygiene.

PRELUDE TO SOAP

To cleanse the mind: a little piece of soap. Suffice it to be well-handled. Where a gush of clear water would remove nothing. Neither would silence. Nor your suicide in the furthest reaches of the dark source, most orthodox reader.

Living underneath the water-pump is worth nothing beyond a hiccough. And a triumph of absurdity would be to stand with arms crossed, up to the waist in water that gushes on towards the Dead Sea.

Trust me, the smallest bowl would be more effective . . . Now, watch him under the tap rubbing like mad to make the soap speak.

Up to this point, with the text being enunciated carefully and hand-written with an eye to style, it seemed to me to be sufficiently substantial to be forwarded to my two closest friends, Albert Camus and Jean Paulhan.

I have not yet received a reply from Paulhan. From Camus this soon arrived:

"Whereas your intentions are usually transparent, as far as soap goes they escape me a little: with so much left out I cannot become aware of the whole. Without washing anything away could you perhaps grease the hinges a little and oil the conjunctions. That said, you must make no alteration to the text. But there again, you see it more clearly than I do. All of which raises one big problem: in my experience real control of style is dependent upon a sense of abandon from time to time. Your sense of abandon has tended to be irony, but irony leaves things out. That is why reading your texts gives the reader the impression that you have invaded his sensibilities and justified the scaling of the heights of his intelligence.

But your *Twelve Little Scripts* permitted me to witness a different style of abandon in your work, one which I should like to see repeated from time to time (it is for that reason that I have particular regard for *the Pebble* amongst your study of trees). Of course, I say 'from time to time' because this does not constitute the centre of your art. That is to be found in what you choose to do, which you achieve with perfection."

✱

Paulhan's silence and the caution of Camus gave me much to ponder upon, and I arrived, little by little, at the decision, in order to make my writerly intentions as clear as possible without, however, making any alteration to the text, with which I was thoroughly happy, without adding anything, even the smallest phrase, the tiniest word, to invent a sort of textual distribution of the different propositions (grammatically speaking) of which it is composed.

A sort of distribution of parts similar to the manner in which a stage-director (the person who in your own terms might be referred to as the Producer*) hands out the text, for which he has taken responsibility for rehearsing for an audience, to different actors and different voices.*

I insist that my text itself will be in no sense altered. It is merely a matter of placing it within a dramatic context.

And here is what I arrived at for the beginning of the summer in 1944.

Camus, who was deeply involved with the theatre at this time, and whom I had informed by letter of my intentions (after all he was in Paris at this time helping out with the staging for a private performance of Picasso's The Devil Caught by the Tail*), urged me to pull together this little dramatic amuse-bouche, Soap. However, having finished it, I didn't have the opportunity to send it to him given the state of France early in that summer of 1944.*

So here is what I arrived at purely for myself:

SOAP

[continues]

LEWIS PORTER

Concerto for Saxophone, for Dave Liebman

Movement 2

In Memoriam Corinne Mond

Copyright © Lewis Porter 2012

The premiere of this movement, featuring Dave Liebman with
Harvard's Dudley House Orchestra, conducted by Aaron Kuan
19 April 2012 is posted with the composer's program notes at
https://youtu.be/vOF4WLOZS3w

Movement 2: In Memoriam Corona Maisal (1962-2011)

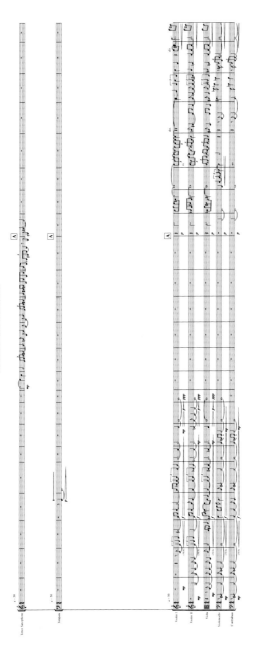

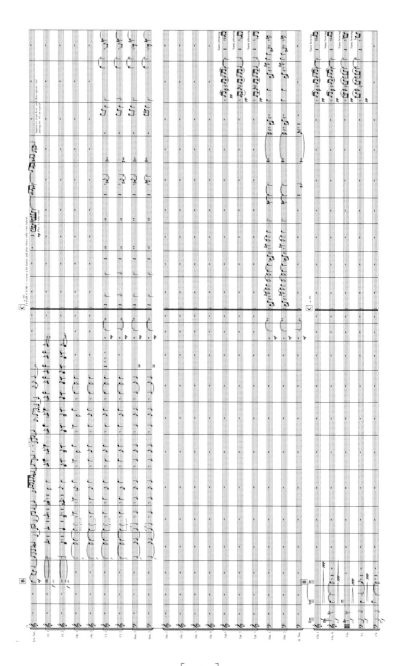

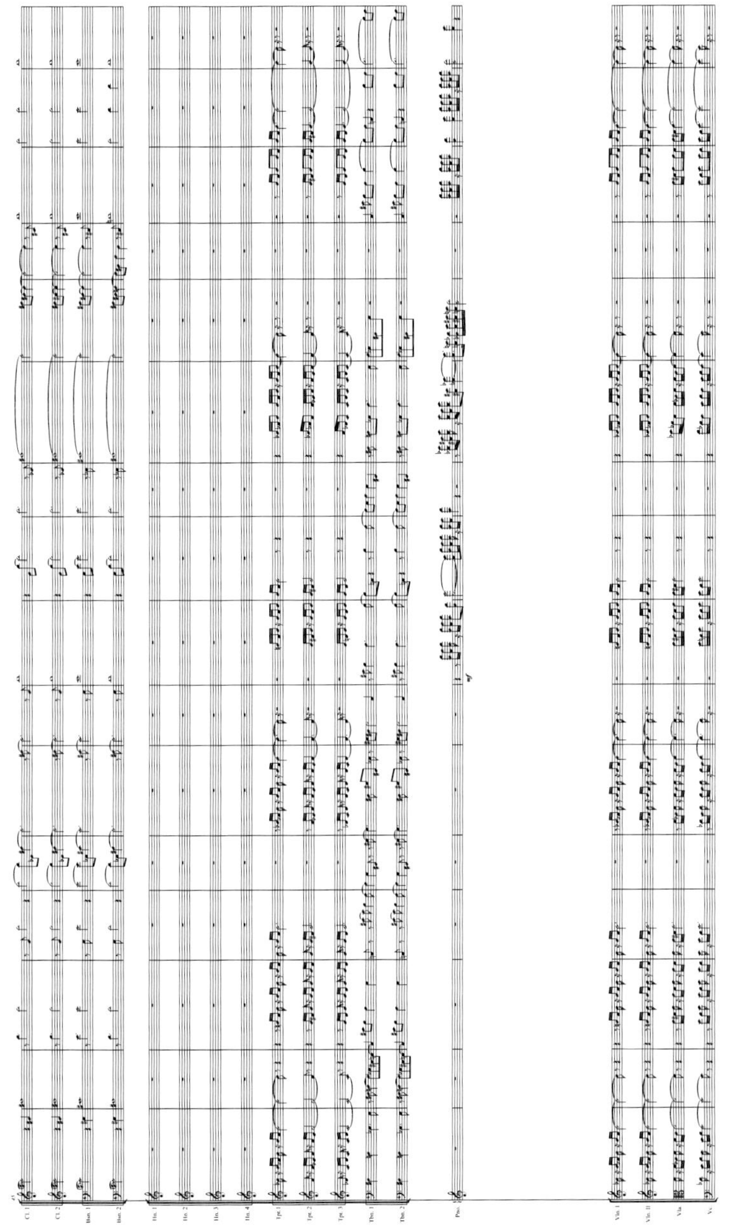
Cl. 1
Cl. 2
Bsn. 1
Bsn. 2
Hn. 1
Hn. 2
Hn. 3
Hn. 4
Tpt. 1
Tpt. 2
Tpt. 3
Tbn. 1
Tbn. 2
Pno.
mf
Vln. I
Vln. II
Vla.
Vc.

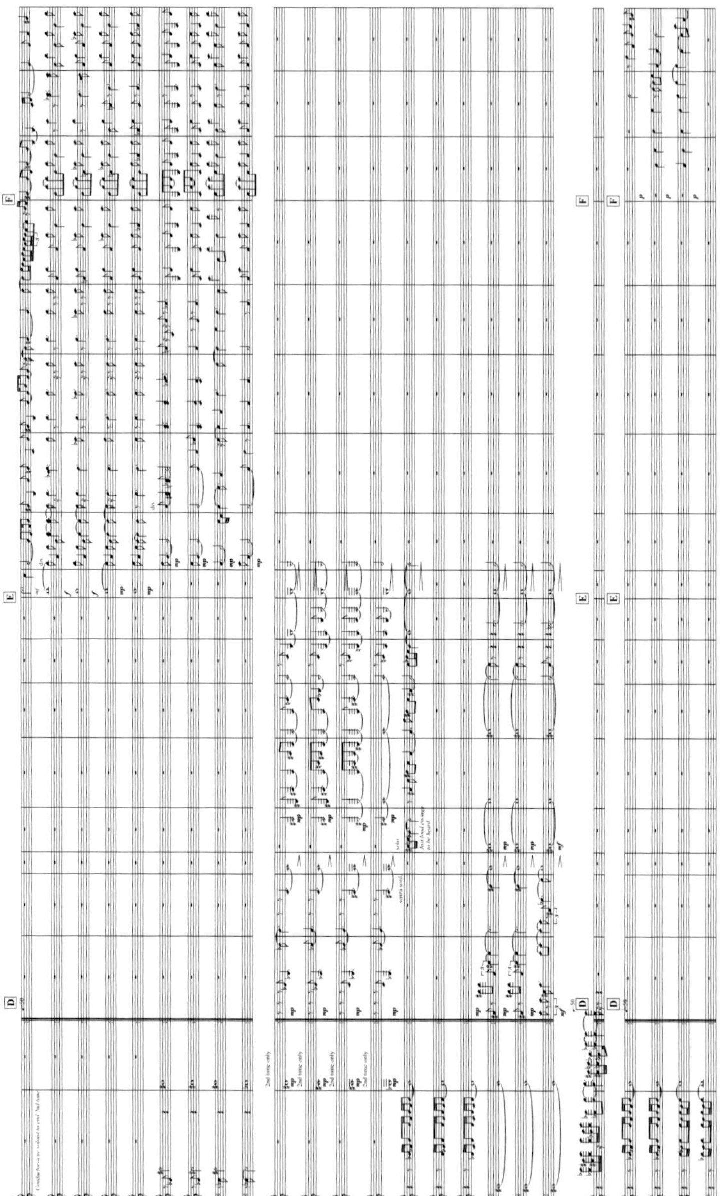
Fl. 1
Fl. 2
Ob. 1
Ob. 2
Cl. 1
Cl. 2
Bsn. 1
Bsn. 2
Hn. 1
Hn. 2
Hn. 3
Hn. 4
Tpt. 1
Tpt. 2
Tpt. 3
Tbn. 1
Tbn. 2
B. Tbn.
Pno.
Vln. I
Vln. II
Vla.
Vc.
D
E
F

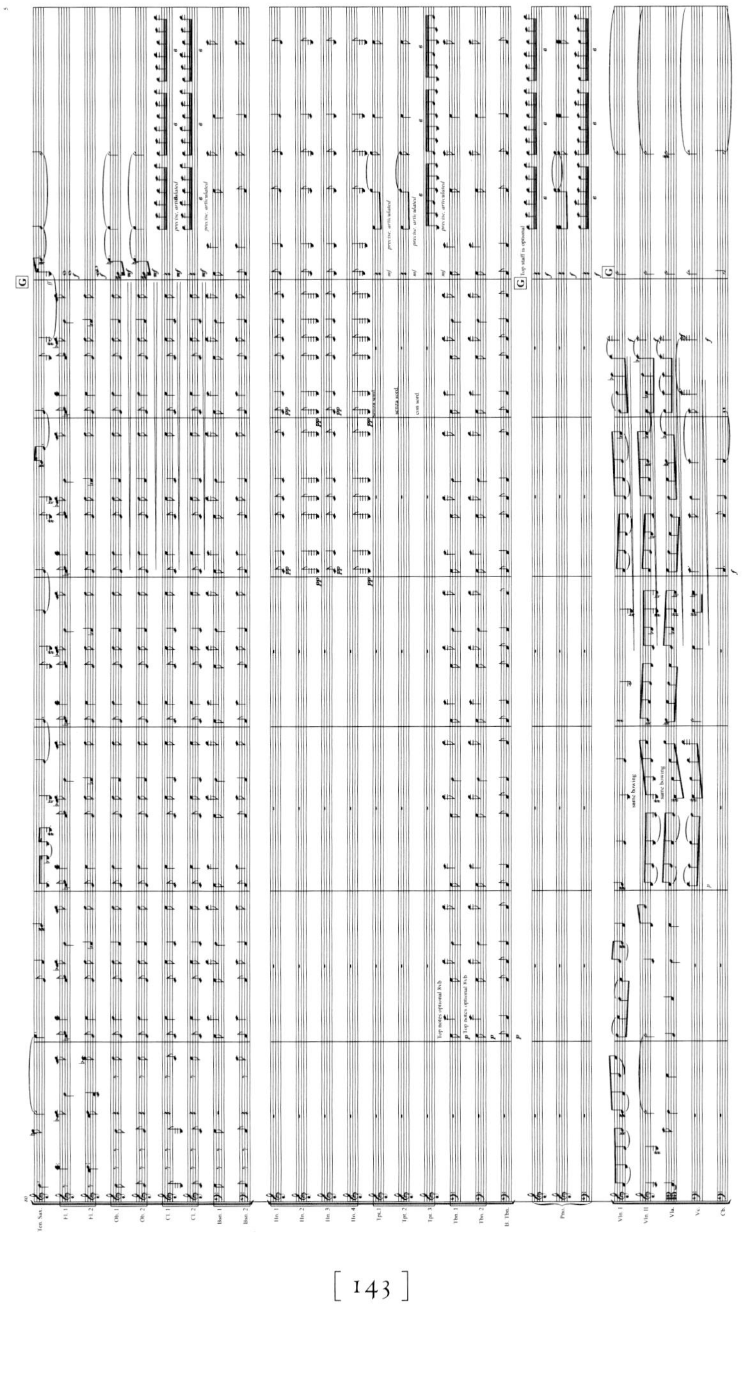
Ten. Sax.
Fl. 1
Fl. 2
Ob. 1
Ob. 2
Cl. 1
Cl. 2
Bsn. 1
Bsn. 2
Hn. 1
Hn. 2
Hn. 3
Hn. 4
Tpt. 1
Tpt. 2
Tpt. 3
Tbn. 1
Tbn. 2
B. Tbn.
Pno.
Vln. I
Vln. II
Vla.
Vc.
Cb.
G
precise, articulated
senza sord.
con sord.
Top notes optional 8vb
Top staff is optional
same bowing

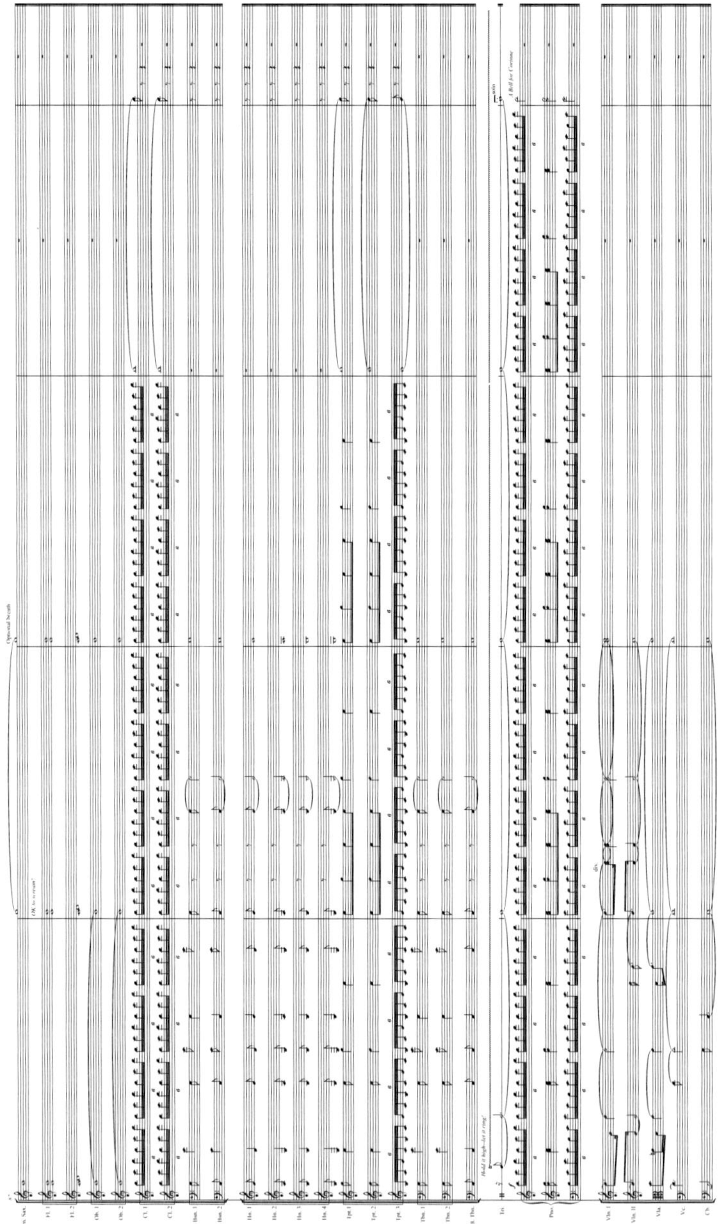
Ten. Sax.
Fl. 1
Fl. 2
Ob. 1
Ob. 2
Cl. 1
Cl. 2
Bsn. 1
Bsn. 2
Hn. 1
Hn. 2
Hn. 3
Hn. 4
Tpt. 1
Tpt. 2
Tpt. 3
Tbn. 1
Tbn. 2
B. Tbn.
Ten.
Pno.
Vln. I
Vln. II
Vla.
Vc.
Cb.
Oh, to scream!
Optional breath
Hold it high--let it ring!
solo
A Bell for Corinne
div.

GEORGES RODENBACH

translated from the French by

WILL STONE

The Graves

It was a very old graveyard and had been abandoned. There were little more than a few headstones still standing, as if the graves themselves had also perished. As in their turn the graves die out above the dead, a still more sorrowful dejection persists like tears spun in rain.

Here and there amongst the thick grass, a few more grave slabs show through. But so worn, so ancient! They have lost their inscription as an old grandmother her memory.

In particular there are three next to one another, exactly alike. It seems they were destined for three sisters.

But one has already given up, keeling over into the grass.

The two remaining stones remain upright and steadfast; giving the impression that each hammers on a door which merely opens onto complete nothingness, above an utterly mouldered corpse.

The inclining stone on the other hand would seem to signal a more definite ending, that death might be restored to the earth, which is indeed bruised and swollen there as if burgeoned by the exact space taken by a body and enriched by the nourishment of decomposition.

But it was saddening to reflect that one of the three sisters was 'even more dead'.

What confirmed this impression was a butterfly fluttering about the more degraded tomb. It was white and black, the colour of the procession of virgins. It lingered with an uncertain flutter, as if dazzled to be finally free and solitary in the naked air.

Doubtless it was born in this particular tomb, which was why it seemed able to leave it only under duress.

Was this the soul itself, only liberated at that moment? Does the soul remain with the body much longer than one imagines? Is the one interred along with the other? Does it not endure, invisible, to spin the spider's web of dream in the slumber of death as in the slumber of night? Perhaps it too descends into the grave, clings stubbornly to the corpse like a ship to water, and only departs later, at the last moment, when finally all the flesh has dissolved, all matter is trans-substantiated and only the futile wreckage of the bones is left . . . ?

That moment then was the fulfillment of the interred virgin beneath her leaning stone. So, the white butterfly was her soul departing, yet still suspended and lingering over memories, above the clay which had appropriated the form of the extinct body.

In the old abandoned graveyard, there is also a great tomb set against the surrounding wall, a massive sarcophagus already virtually derelict. The names and dates have wasted away and perished one by one, as if death itself was obliterated by death . . . The stones return to their natural state. A curtailed destiny for these stones that acquire their identity for a fleeting moment, as equally their passing. They were tombs once, richly embellished with crowns, they were marveled at in the anonymous throng of tombs and humble crosses, whose outstretched arms seem like those of a beggar.

For a long time the sarcophagus prevailed.

Now it is restored to an impersonal stone, a frivolous mineral. Only an urn, at its side, endures in the integrity of its form.

It was as if the soul of this body of stone, had emerged from it like the white butterfly from its body of flesh and bone.

Curvilinear, it seemed almost to be taking off. This was the most agile and aerial object realised from stone.

An airborne urn, you would think it really was hovering there for a moment above the mighty sarcophagus of which it was but a part, likewise grey in colour, and that at long last was taking its leave, ceasing to be itself, and already seeming more like an anonymous stone than that of the tomb.

The few surviving headstones, embedded in the earth like anchors, stood erect and tall amongst the jaded grass.

Forsaken and left to itself, the grass was fading, tangled up with the jumble of hair belonging to the dead, hair that was no longer combed.

In this disorder of vegetation, the gravestones loom up, unyielding, geometric.

Nothing could disturb them. Even the winds of the October storms are impotent, as if merely pounding on the door of eternity.

The sun alone thwarted their impassiveness; as, in spite of them, their shadow varied, moving around them. According to the sun's position the grave was now in shadow and now in sunlight. The interlude of light and dark! A pall of darkness over the grave then suddenly one of golden light! As if death had in turn opened and closed its eyes.

The old graveyard was denuded, one by one, of all its graves.

Nothing now remains but a vast livid lawn, whose ashen pallor proves to be the old destination. None cares for such a dejected plot and has no wish to site their home upon the recollections of bones. Death has proved too obstinate an owner to allow this fold to be reconciled with life.

Now in the midst of this empty solitude at the place where the three standing headstones are, for those sisters side by side, somehow a beautiful lily peers through.

It rises up, white as snow or linen, above the grassy tussocks, like the cup of silence . . . to display those rounded edges, this languid nodding, doubtless influenced by the stone urn that vanished, but is recognised once more here in the bloom.

Or perhaps it has taken its dull pastel whiteness from the butterfly which also vanished and yet is seen in the flower.

Eternal metempsychosis!

At the same time it is the urn which seemed to be the body of stone that was the sarcophagus, and the butterfly which appeared to be the soul of the interred body. It has the form of the urn and the colour of the butterfly.

Bell-like white lily, that symbolizes the fallen graveyard! Lily that rises from the grave, but signifies life! As, sprouting from the place where the three dead sisters lie, it unfurls, opens out like one great unviolated sex, this lily verging on the carnal, flower that proclaims the invincible force of matter and the chemical fecundity of death.

————

Les Tombeaux, 1895

MIKLÓS RADNÓTI

translated from the Hungarian by

MARK SOMOS

selected from the complete
Radnóti Miklós, *Összes versei és versfordításai*, ed. Pál Réz
Budapest, Szépirodalmi Könyvkiadó, 1984

PSALMS OF DEVOTION

1

Between our torn, upset lips even the
spinning, straining words are banished,
rounding into kisses here between the
ornate eyelashes in our interlocked
admiring eyes and they die without
making a sound; what they are born
on to is a sumptuous gift, a hymnal
vision and the winged, clapping embrace of
yellow orioles on a wise kiss's broad trunk.

27 August 1929

2

Bright stars snatched
long ago want to flee
my fingers' grasp
because I love you very much
   you see
my life's mood is stretched taut
on swelling berry clusters of
autumn bushes, I feel the burdens
of ripe corns in the ear
and each night
I kiss mutely upon your palm
the twilight red
of my tongue, prone to kiss.

10 December 1928

3

The domed fingers of your cool sometimes
sweltering hot hand are the musical spires
of my slender life which is as rich
in vaporous colours as our bountiful kisses
in the silence when followed
by your lace-adorned sighing gasps and
the love-struck shiver of my big wet teeth.

26 May 1928

4

The orange that shines like gold in your
delicate fingers is our lives' old ardour
because we admired once together the
hot, colourful birds building nests as they sang
at the bottom of drizzling, miraculous groves.

On the hollow of your palm hot groves
tell tales of abandoned skies
from which we tumbled together
two white innocent virgins, marvelous
flowers already bloomed in the bud:
for our wonderful heavenly child was
conceived without embrace into
the lap of forests, leafy and deciduous.

7 February 1929

5

Now, as in a new god from blue skies
sweet-tuned pipe organs boom inside of me,
my dream mountains crumble one by one,—
you've come to me now fallen like
the stars in the autumn, because I love you so
bearing in my eyes the infinite lives of
white-bearded gods and
I learn your kisses
as a believer!
the way old women learn fortune-telling with cards.

25 June 1929

6

Only our nails' pale half-moon shines
and lowering the heavy curtain of our eyes
we play love with our blind hands, because
purple birds are sitting in the mist
under the streetlights, and should we open them
walls of mist would part in our mute eyes and
only the half-moon of our nails would shine on.

5 March 1929

7

Sometimes we bite. On the armour
of our bright teeth the kiss breaks with a snap
and a garland of tiny blood drops
flutters toward our brow.
A star crawls and crawls
on the sky and under our love
the grass bends with a curtsy, hedgerows
hold, hold on in the wind
as do the tongues of sometimes gentle lovers
stick together when, in kissing, they touch.

9 July 1929

8

You are an earth-smelling meadow, your panting simple
like a sharecropper's who makes love and your
body bears the accursed strength of mother earth.
At times only your desire's bell rings me
and calls me to Mass in the breathing silence
under the tower of darkness panting.
Your love spirals down on me like a falling
great wild chestnut tree leaf. Even now.
At sorrow's translucent clear dawn
you are the earth, the body, the blood
and everything other than you is a game.

12 July 1928

FUNERAL SONG

In the old woman, in whose house I live,
I think the woman has died yesterday
night, because on the morning as loud as she could
she sang, standing long over her bed and
now like a child, she sneaks among the solemn
tulips in the garden and leaves her mouth
agape when the wind, frightened, brings from the road
a young bouquet of the voices of lads fooling around
with girls, but perhaps the grapes in the arbour
will ripen ten more times, before she completely dies.

8 May 1930

POPPY

My woman notices a poppy
and whistles to me across the road
and as I whistle back, she bends down.

Her two fingers slide through the stem's
hairs and stop among the grass. And at once
the gossamer flower is flaming in her hand.

I whistle again; into my whistle a happy
bird's whistle mingles and she smiles:
Let the world start a riot of poppy-flower red!

13 June 1933

TWENTY-EIGHT YEARS

Aggressive, hideous baby was I,
twin-bearing mommy,—your killer!
Whether you delivered my brother stillborn,
or he lived five minutes, I don't know,
but there amid the blood and wailing
they lifted me toward the light
like a victorious, little wild brute,
who already showed what he was worth:
two dead behind him.

Two dead behind me,
the world before me,
I grew up from such depth
as the thugs;
I grew up as an orphan,
from the depths, to here,
the ringing, harsh
freedom's spacious and
windswept roof tops.

How deep was my childhood,
and how chilly.
Instead of your call a snake
hissed at me in my games'
little paths, when evening fell
I saw blood on my pillows
instead of the big, snow white fluff
that frightens the child.

How deep was my childhood,
and how tall the youth!
Were the two deaths worth it?—
I shouted at the picture,
which shone on my room's wall.
You were twenty-eight *then*,
maybe twenty-five on the picture,
a solemn young woman,
serious-looking, brooding.

You were twenty-eight *then*,
I just turned the same age,
twenty-eight years you've been dead,
mommy! bloody fugitive!

Mommy, bloody sacrifice,
I grew up into manhood,
the sun beats down heavily, blinding
wave to me with your butterfly hand
that it's alright like this, that *you* understand,
and I'm not alive in vain.

May 1937

GUARD AND PROTECT ME

In my dream the wind blows at nights
and the sails flashing white
are swelling with a snap, prepared for a long journey.

I'm writing this slow verse here
like a man who says goodbyes, and starts his life again,
from then on to write his poems with a stick
on the hovering sands of faraway Africa.

But from everywhere, even Africa,
horrible crying is heard; its frightening
child the wet-nurse time suckles day and night
from her purple-blue breasts.

What value have words between two wars,
and what am I worth, expert in rare and
difficult words, if moronically
every giddy hand is clutching a bomb!

Flames run up on our sky and on our land falls
the reader of signs in celestial light,
pain encircles me whitely,
like salt surrounds the sea at low tide.

Guard and protect me, white-blazing pain
and you, snow-coloured consciousness, stay with me:
let not my clean word ever be tarnished
with the fear that burns with a brown smoke!

1937

KAT PEDDIE

COAST: TANKERTON—SEASALTER

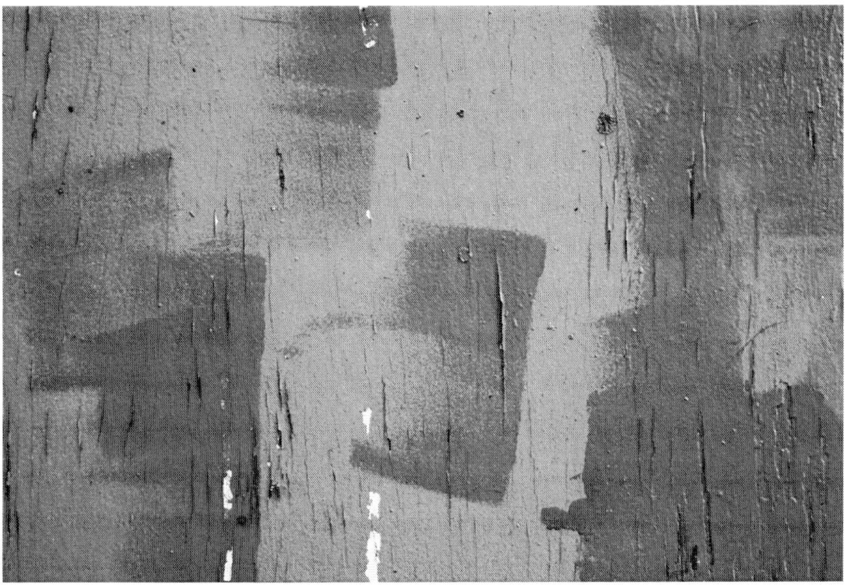

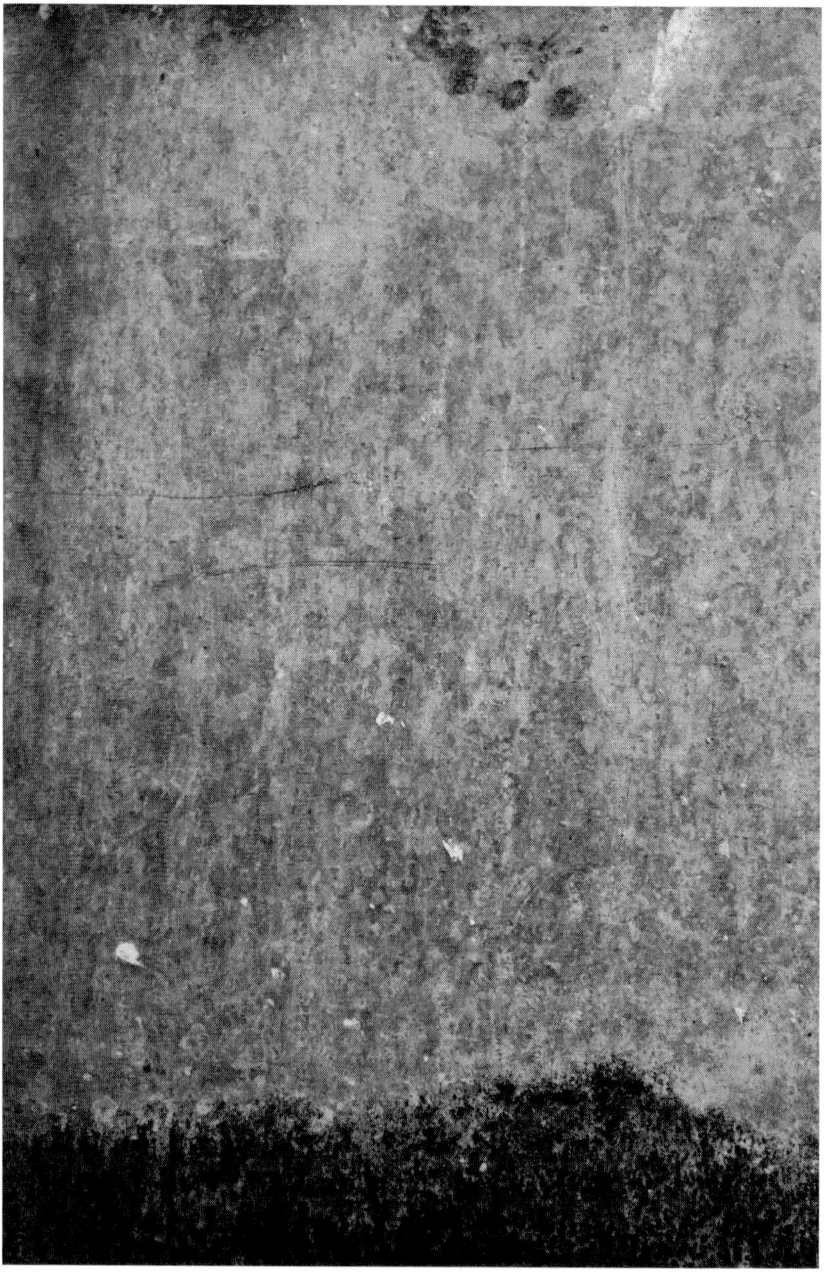

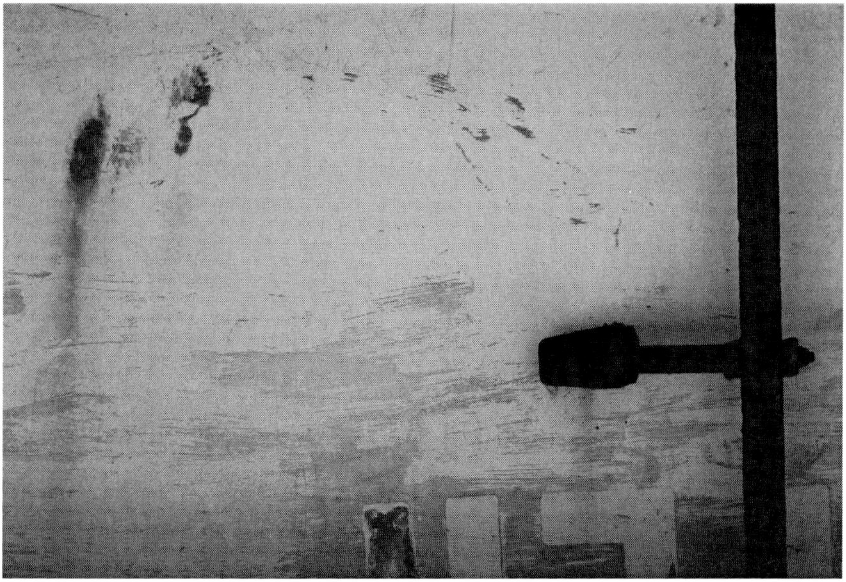

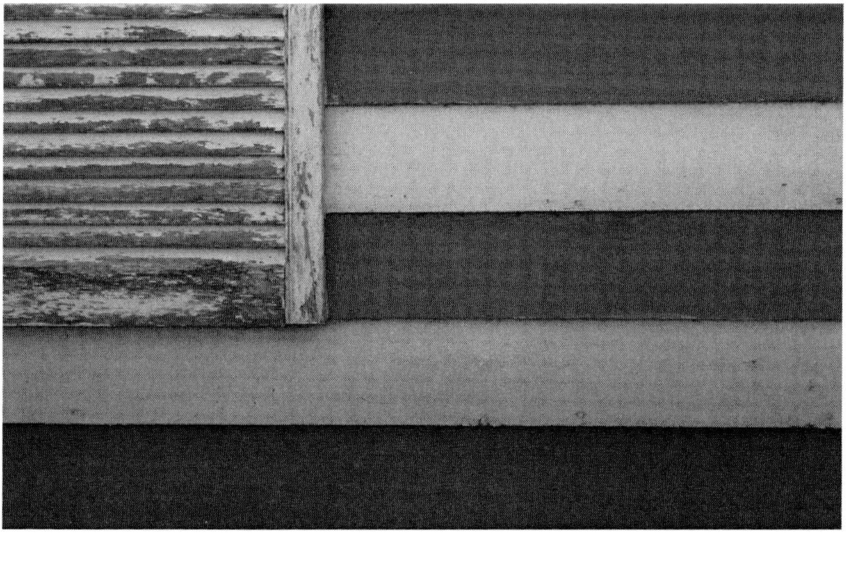

ANON

BALLAD OF THE LOST MITTEN

translated from the Old Norwegian by

A CHILDE

With wool my love   she knitted me
    Two mittens green in hue.
Wings of a dove   they fitted me
    And warmed my fingers through.

Refrain: O the kitten

I had to go   away somewhere
    For no more than a day.
The winds can blow   so fiercely there
    A mitten blew away.

I asked the one   who said to me
    "I'm Keeper of the Green"
If on its own   like this you see
    A mitten there had been.

I held it up   and turned it out
    For everyone around.
"I cannot sup   nor move about
    Unless it can be found."

Nearby was spied   beneath a tree
    A leather gauntlet glove.
"But no!" I cried. "That cannot be.
    It was a gift of love."

[164]

There came a shout   from bearded mouth
    A fellow waved his hand.
"Without a doubt   the wind blew south
    'Tis in another land."

Then came a shout   as I went forth
    A lassie waved her hand.
"Without a doubt   the wind blew north
    'Tis in that other land."

I bade farewell   and setting stride
    I wished for I were there.
And on a fjell   I stood beside
    My lovely lady fair.

"So sweet, so fair   you are quite dark
    I love you all the same.
I'm in despair   this is no lark
    I cannot hide my shame."

"A mitten still   you have not lost
    I thank the Lord above.
You know my will   there is no cost
    For I shall be your love."

A mitten more   she knitted me
    Then put away the thread.
She shut the door   she turned the key
    And led me to her bed.

O the kitten

———

Rural dialect ballad, also known in a variant translatable as "Song of the Green Glove"
probably dating from the late eighteenth century and first recorded in *Norske Folkeviser:
Samlede og udgivne af M. B. Landstad*, suppl. (Christiania, Christian Tønsbergs Forlag, 1853)

MARA MALANOVA

translated from the Russian by

KSENIA GOLUBOVICH

& CAROLINE CLARK

Poems

How good it is to go far away,
so far that time itself is no more,
it was only yesterday that milk was spilt in the heavens,
and a horse rider's foot stuck in his stirrup.
How good it is to stay and not to leave,
not to abandon your old place,
and to try on another life,
like a bride with a white dress.
How good it is to stay and not to die,
and hope for morning,
since at night an army of snowflakes will come,
or rain will fall from the heavens
like Brahmaputra from the Himalayas.

The one who'll break our heart
Will be the most loved,
It is but from his hands that we'll want to take the cure,
And the heart will soon forget the pain he has caused,
For what is love if not the very name of cunning.

Have no regrets,
Have no things to keep,
Days fly away
Like doves from the roof,
And the sky grows empty
Like a house abandoned,
And the blood grows chill:
For I know this world—
From the Polar Star to a fleck of dust
On an old Rembrandt canvas,
What remains is to celebrate
The wake for its terrible beauty.

One more year and all will change,
All will change for the hundredth time,
The hidden tree will break out in foliage,
And damp earth will cover a manhole
Into the past that will not let me go,
As if I were its own dead.
One more year and the snow will melt on my eyelashes
And the death-mask will fall from my face.

It seemed there was no more to wait for,
That fate had been generous at the start,
And now the time had come to pack up and leave,
And the glass had no more wine,
Yet still the blood was stirring
From the world that's flying by,
And life is like a child's love—
First unknown, then inexhaustible.

It seems that
it is possible
to flap one's hands and disappear,
to see a window in a mirror,
reject all names,
and drifting over the hill,
sliding over the river,
to say goodbye for one last time
to that old dream
that once was me.

You cannot fall asleep from happiness,
from sorrow you cannot waken,
the soul is trembling like quick-silver
in its attempts to smile,
like a beast fleeing the hunter,
invisible in its own dark,
and right till the end
it will not believe
that it is immortal.

Coast

An arrow, having reached its target, trembles a while, then settles. A man, having reached his goal, rejoices a while, then sets off in search of a new one, or seized by a sudden fit of sorrow he stares aimlessly at the horizon.

Assol

From time to time a wind blows in from the future,
and the heart starts beating like waves against the shore,
and the eyes make something out in the distance.

Give me a black stone,
Put it in my right hand
And let my guardian who knows no sleep
Turn into thy shadow.

Give me a strong shroud,
Cast my death away,
And from the quiet regions of my temple
Wipe the mirror's dust.

And that pauper soul of mine
Will lose all memory of you
Only when, a stranger even unto me,
It is hurrying to its far-off abode.

HEAD TO HEAD

The earth still holds you
and the sky keeps an eye on you.
But your enemy too
is held by the earth,
and the sky does not turn away from him.
It's only in the fight
that you'll realize
how cold the earth is,
how indifferent the sky.

I had a dream as open as a gallery,
A herd of horses was flying through the steppe,
And the steed threw off the herdsman,
A horrid wind was howling over the earth,
And my heart was crumbling like rotten wood.
But there was something akin between the wind
And the emptiness gaping in my breast,
Such a honey-sweet force
And the unknown ahead.

love does not feed on carrion
it wears out slowly
falls
a shadow on the neighbour's house
and familiar music swirls through the air
shakes the trees
throws leaves to the wind

love does not feed on carrion
it wears out slowly
falls
comes down to earth
the sky flashes with
lightning
thunder
and the earth shatters

love does not feed on carrion
it wears out
slowly
falls
water from the heavens

YEAR

Winter lingers,
spring steps out,
summer's full stride,
autumn arrives.

TACTIC

A boy was telling a story about his sister.
Once they were eating pirozhki in the kitchen.
Suddenly his sister saw a cockroach.
She pressed a finger to her lips
and said: "Shhh . . .
let's take the pirozhki
and quietly
tiptoe away . . ."

You wake up and it's winter outside the window.
While that soul of yours was wandering far away,
the world has changed.
I open my eyes and hear your voice:
Snow makes the wind visible.

there are all sorts of words
some have a rough
offensive crust
others are like soapy spheres
they drift from our heads
someplace upwards
then sideways
and there are caught
by the verbal god
he knows them inside out
chokes on them
and is struck dumb
but still he loves all sorts of words
for they make the feet dance
and the head swirl

ISAI KALASHNIKOV

translated from the Russian by

KSENIA GOLUBOVICH

& CAROLINE CLARK

from

CRUEL AGE

Hoelun sat down and looked around the yurt. By the wall facing the entrance there was a narrow table with leather puppets on it—*ongon*—with
greasy heads, the traces of sacrificial food. And a second table by the
hearth bearing bowls and a large earthen vessel. In the hearth under the
black, smoky cauldron there was a pile of coal and ash; and another table,
quite small, with a glossy black lid and carved legs, standing at her bed-
side on the snow-white embroidered felt rug. Her bed is in the eastern
half of the yurt; there is another bed opposite hers by the fireplace, but
it is empty; close to the entrance there are clothes hanging on the wall,
armor made of thick cowhide, and an old, battered and worn quiver. All
things familiar to her from childhood, except the black table, so brilliant,
its lid could be used as a mirror. She is seeing it for the first time. Where
is she? What will happen to her? She has remembered her Chiledu and
silently weeps. He is probably already dead. She had promised to save
him and did not. She too must die.

—

Temujin wasn't sure whether Togoril had given a sign or whether the storm of riders tore away by themselves. Hoofbeats thundered the ears and a cloud of thick dust flew up into the sky. The riders were racing as if on the run from that grey cloud. Black arrows showered from the ranks of the Merkids, and the ranks began to move and then rushed forward. Temujin was swinging his sword and shouting, unable to hear his own voice. The rider on a russet wide-chested steed was flying at him, pointing the spearhead at his chest. Temujin rolled to the side of the saddle and the spear missed him. Jelme's sword flashed like lighting and crashed down on the head of a Merkid. The Merkids were fighting fiercely and courageously, pushing forward harder and harder. The Khan's warriors stopped and then retreated. It seemed to Temujin that the Khan's army would soon be overpowered. Fearing this and powerless to change a thing, he started to look around for Togoril. But all he could see in the clouds of grey dust was the flashing of fierce foreign faces and the snarling snouts of the horses. Iron was clanging, hoofs were pounding, human death cries were merging with the mad neighing of horses. For a moment it seemed to him that the Khan and his blood brother had thrown him under the swords of the Merkids. Fear muddled his mind. Temujin was tearing at the reins to turn the horse back. His only wish was to gallop away as far as possible from that tangle of human hatred. But Jelme was on his right and Boorchu on his left. He was clamped between them.

—

He went back into the woods. He built a shelter out of twigs and grass and climbed in. He got warm and fell asleep. Bird song woke him. He stuck his head out of the shelter. The rain had stopped. The sky had cleared, the sun was shining bright. Raindrops were hanging from the leaves and pine needles, sparkling with bright colours. It was late afternoon. He had a terrible hunger. He got up and walked along the hillside. He needed to get closer to the yurt. At night he might succeed in seeing some of his own.

—

Why do the heavens give everything to some and nothing to others? He does not want gold or fame or glory. He would settle for just a yurt, a horse, a couple dozen sheep and a bit of freedom. Nothing else. No, he would want Kaimish to be by his side. And her grandfather too. In the evenings they would sit and talk by the fire and dry straight pliant twigs of hargana. Is that too much? Oh heavens ever blue, and benevolent spirits, help me get all I wish for!

—

translated from the edition of *Zhestoki Vek* (1978)
published by Khankhakaev Gallery, Moscow, 2010

the order of the appearance of these four extracts in
the original is "Hoelun", "Why", "Temujin", "He"

ANTHONY BARNETT

SETTLED BY DOVES

THIS SNOW LEAF IS SETTLED BY DOVES, NOT CENTAURS, the latter being *Snow*'s, indeed ABP's generally, preferred house font. Dear Centaur, whether you are male or female, do not chastise me for abandoning you to take shape for a moment in a different flight of fancy. You are not so far apart in that you both have the oblique e-stroke I like, whatever your other Venetian Jenson serif derived differences may be, indeed are. Quite. You Doves are remarkably grounded considering your escapades—to put it ~~muddily~~ mildly—in The Thames, while you Centaur are quite, how shall I put it, escapably, escapadably, fleet of foot.

Here in a nutshell is the infamous famous story. A century ago, the partners in the Doves Press, Thomas Cobden-Sanderson and Emery Walker, fell out. From 1916, over three years of nights, Cobden-Sanderson consigned the complete fount, punches, matrices and metal, to its watery grave off the Hammersmith Bridge so that no one would ever again be able to print books in his beautiful 16pt type, cut by Edward Prince. In 2013, Robert Green of Typespec, Manchester, revived the Doves Press Roman in a digital facsimile, based on original books and ephemera. Not content, in 2014 Green embarked on an expedition with Port of London Authority divers, recovering a portion of the lost metal. In early 2015 he reissued the type in a more precise version, which is, mostly, what you are reading here. Why mostly?* The original Doves Type was roman only, without italic or small caps. Typespec's release is true to that, while adding some new glyphs and diacritics. When Doves Press printed in italic it used Edinburgh foundry Miller & Richard Old Style. No digital so-called Old Style italic fits at all satisfactorily with Doves.

Assiduous research reveals that Swedish typographer Torbjörn Olsson designed and issued a version of Doves Type in 1994–1995, evidently updated

---

*Distinct features of Doves Type include dropped opening " 'quotes' ", and curtailed ſ and markedly offset i tittle, both true to 1470 Jenson, absent or attenuated in almost all revivals and derivations

2002, based on his study of Doves Press print. Olsson is hard to track down: email addresses bounce back; the Swedish firm T4 through which a few of his types are sold does not list Doves. What is more, The Doves Type® is now a name registered by Typespec. Don't ask me how but I have got hold of Olsson's version. If it was the only Doves revival in existence it would be good but Green's, Green's first version even, is more faithful and better proportioned, the more so in light of studying original metal—in the roman. Where Olsson's version comes into its own is in his inclusion of newly designed italic and small caps, and alternate lining figures also not present in the original or in Green—see the figure 4 in the second line of this page—with some new glyphs and ornaments, to accompany his roman. The first line, and *Snow* and ABP, in the second line of the previous page, and now here, are set in Olsson's version, in adjusted pointing. To have a more than reasonable accompanying *italic*—see also below—is a boon. To forego SMALL CAPS digitally generated from roman for true SMALL CAPS so designed is useful too.

Thank you, Centaur, an olive branch

Typespec The Doves Type® *has roman discretionary ligature &*
http://www.typespec.co.uk/doves-type/
http://www.typespec.co.uk/doves-type-revival/
http://www.typespec.co.uk/recovering-the-doves-type/

Olsson Doves Type Pro *has roman & italic discretionary ligatures & & &*
http://home.swipnet.se/~w-10011/Tobbe/Tobbe.html
http://luc.devroye.org/fonts-27212.html

Marianne Tidcombe, *The Doves Press* (London, British Library, & New Castle, DE, Oak Knoll, 2002 [2003]), comprehensive history, set in Galliard CC, a non-oblique-e type first issued 1978, based on 16th-c. Granjon
Simon Garfield, *Just My Type: A Book About Fonts* (London, Profile, 2010), 90–94, chap. "Doves", lay account

Bruce Rogers, *Paragraphs on Printing: Elicited from Bruce Rogers in Talks with James Hendrickson on the Functions of the Book Designer* (New York, Rudge, 1943; fascimile repr. New York, Dover, 1979), c.100 illus., set in 1932 MT recut of 1788, then 1930 MT, Bell, a non-oblique-e type used by Rogers at the Riverside Press in 1900
Bruce Rogers, *The Centaur Types* (Chicago, October, 1949; facsimile repr. West Lafayette, IN, Purdue Univ., 1996), illus. account of the type, first cut 1914, recut 1929 MT; Rogers visited England 1916, the year Doves Type began to meet its fate, working first with Doves' Emery Walker, then as advisor to CUP, 1917–1919
Joseph Blumenthal, *Bruce Rogers: A Life in Letters, 1870–1957* (Austin, TX, Taylor, 1989)
Jerry Kelly, & Misha Beletsky, *The Noblest Roman: A History of the Centaur Types of Bruce Rogers* (Rochester, NY, RIT, 2015), incl. new research into unpublished papers

The dove ornaments above are two of several in black & white in Olsson Doves Type Pro
The olive branch is from the Author

JULIET TROY

WILT

1.

We crawl out through morning to greet halos listen to crow caw from
chimney pots breeze through morning paper   intermittent drawl of
people walking past sky transmutes from pink to blue   early birds
still navigate rolling nimbostrati   slip into edge feathered between
here and air   flies he is talking to   you plant a bunch of seed pods
hanging to trunk foliate limb across the heath footpaths threading past
snapped wood where light luminescent algae tips twigs on the path
in the forest   flesh   sap running root   scratch of branch   touches
through barbellate fern

2.

you crush another landscape pose into hovering shape could a green
vote have changed order of the genera?   people in a crowd   hold genetic
memory   photographic traces   my memory hawk moths against
luminosity   transubstantiation of shadow to petalling   a green to leaf
apex   soft light exposure   ambient light   living on the lithosphere
network of paths woodpecker drumming

3.

turbulence through grass   willows tree limbs tormentose   spiegel pond
glance reveals tall plants leaning in the breeze   leaves oblong-lanceolate
flowers ultra-fragile inflorescence long   I hold markers   calculate the
spread of patch   blue orchids strange walking plants   seed pod
dissemination   hot breath misting into act   Gaultier's Brides on the
catwalk snaking through   reproductive organs of a plant   found
fragments of hue   sepal clutch   slashed and split in the wind déjà ils
flétrissent

4.

you follow brocade across bark   I try to decipher   green rhizines
creeping cryptographic   he asks if I'm listening   I think it says 'are
patterning memory of a sky and earth halfway of the plant expanse road
headwind twist and life veins through flower and trunk' while small talk
fell to earth   couches de feuilles mortes   detrital interface   clouds we
are walking through.

ANTHONY BARNETT

Henry Crowder's Letters to Nancy Cunard

We try to fit the pieces together but sometimes there are too many
pieces or there are missing pieces or they might be the wrong shape

IN 2007 I PUBLISHED MY RESEARCH ON THE AFRICAN AMERICAN
pianist who was the consort of Nancy Cunard for some seven years from
1928, *Listening for Henry Crowder: A Monograph on His Almost Lost Music*. At the
time, I had sight of two letters written by Crowder deposited in the Cunard
collection at the Harry Ransom Research Center, University of Texas at
Austin: one dated 3 March 1934, congratulating her on the publication of
Negro: An Anthology, dedicated to Crowder; the other dated 11 August 1954,
thanking her for sending a copy of *Grand Man: Memories of Norman Douglas*,
published that year. I reproduced a brief holograph extract from each of
the letters.

On page 42 I discussed what purported to be two further letters written by Crowder to Cunard, both partly concerning Ezra Pound. One
dated, as we shall see ostensibly, 1952, cited in J. J. Wilhelm, *Ezra Pound:
The Tragic Years, 1925–1972* (1994); the other dated 1953, quoted by Anne
Chisholm in *Nancy Cunard: A Biography* (1979). In fact, Chisholm quoted
from two letters to which she had been given access, the other, not about
Pound, dated November 1954, the 29th as it turns out. In a footnote I
asked why the apparent owner of at least two letters would not reveal
himself or confirm their content, in particular in respect of Pound.

In June 2015, a collection of letters from Crowder to Cunard, laid into
a luxurious modernistic artist-designed album, was the major part of a lot,
one of many, sold at auction by Christie's at the realized price of £6,500 to
publisher and book dealer David Deiss, from the estate of book collector,
authority on Renaissance bindings, and himself an auctioneer, Anthony
Hobson, who died aged ninety-two in 2014. A copy of *Negro* was one of

the other lots. Hobson was Cunard's literary executor and negotiated the sale of some of her papers now at Texas. But about half the Texas Cunard holdings were acquired not from Hobson but from New York book dealer and auctioneer House of El Dieff, no longer in existence. The Texas holdings were the result of a series of purchases between 1969 and 1977. Cunard died in 1965 and Crowder in 1955. Texas is unsure but thinks that their two 1934 and 1954 letters may have been acquired from El Dieff in 1970. How those two letters in particular came to be separated from the rest is an open question but it can be noted that both have a point in common in that they were written in response to receiving books. In light of the album it does seem unreasonable to imagine that Hobson was the one who separated them. Perhaps it was Cunard herself.

I have been able to examine the contents of the tooled-leather album, quite a fetishistic object, commissioned by Hobson from P. L. Martin in 1971. It holds nine letters with five associated envelopes, two notes, two telegrams, three picture postcards with associated envelope, dated 1928 through 1934, and 1953, 1954, the latter two the letters from which Chisholm was able to quote. The earlier letters are mostly passionate declarations of love and longing. The lot also included a few photos of Crowder, Cunard, and both together, none previously unknown.

To return to Wilhelm's 1952 citation: such a letter from Crowder to Cunard cannot exist. Curiously, or significantly, Wilhelm does not include any Crowder letter in his list of correspondence locations. Wilhelm was too ill to talk with by the time I was able to make contact with his daughter while writing my book. His citation, again, significantly, not in quote marks, that Crowder thought Pound crazy as a fox is not to be found in any known Crowder letter. It does not occur in Crowder's description of Pound in the 1953 letter quoted by Chisholm. The wording of that letter makes clear that Crowder and Cunard had not been in contact for "so, so many years". Crowder does goes on to say that he was given a Paris address for Cunard by a fellow pianist but "This was some years ago, and I think I wrote to you, but I am not at all sure."

What, then, is to be made of Wilhelm's 1952 citation? It is certain that Crowder visited Pound at St Elizabeths at least during the latter half of the 1940s. Charles Olson wrote about an occasion when they happened to visit Pound at the same time. I had thought that this could be dated either in the first half of 1946 or on 9 February 1948 but, reviewing the evidence, including the content of 1946 correspondence between Cunard and Pound, it cannot be 1946. It appears that Cunard, after their final mid-1930s break-up, learned of Crowder's post-war whereabouts in 1947. In my book I discuss the circumstances surrounding that period and whether they may have been in touch, which remains very much an open question.

The conclusion seems to be that if Wilhelm had sight of a "crazy as a fox" letter, or was informed of one, his 1952 dating has to be wildly wrong. Much more likely, he has colourfully paraphrased Chisholm's 1953 quotation: "I have a sneaking suspicion that Ezra is putting on an act, and that he is saner than most people." Not, then, the more usual wily as a fox, but crazy as one.

To put it mildly, I am sorry that Hobson's Crowder letters were not available for examination while I was working on my book. They may not have added that much that was terribly important or strictly factual, or not already to be surmised, but to have had some dates and places, including the serendipitous confirmation of a theatre tour, and expressions of passionate or tender affection, with some tiffs, laid bare, would not have gone amiss.

In the posthumously published *As Wonderful As All That? Henry Crowder's Memoir of His Affair with Nancy Cunard, 1928–1935* (1987), Crowder says that in England "I had gotten around the permit question and had secured a fairly decent job in a theatre orchestra." I had surmised a date of 1933 or 1934 and a Buddy Bradley connection, the African American choreographer resident in London with whose brother, Arthur Bradley, Crowder appeared in Paris in 1936. With the Hobson album's three postcards mailed to Cunard in an envelope, postmarked 17 Oct 1934, Dudley, Worcs, in which Crowder writes that he will not be granted a work permit, the matter can now be laid to rest. Crowder's theatre engagement turns out to have been Sam Manning's *The Harlem Night-Birds*, with a black, mainly "British", cast of some thirty-five, which played Dudley Opera House, destroyed in a fire in 1936, for a week from 15 October 1934, two days before Crowder's mailing. The revue opened at Queen's Theatre, Poplar, East London on 24 September, transferring to the Empress Theatre, Brixton, South East London for the week of 1 October, before touring England, Glasgow and Dublin through to the end of May 1935. Birmingham was the first stop before Dudley, and London again immediately after. It is quite on the cards that the dancer Adelaide Willoughly, with whom Crowder had become involved, and with whom he was to tour the Continent in a double act, was one of the show's "12 Dusky Harlem Girls". How long Crowder remained with the show is not known but he was certainly back in France by around spring 1935, in Cambrai, where he and Cunard parted company for good. Trinidadian orchestra leader and comedian Sam Manning, the consort of Amy Ashwood Garvey, estranged first wife of Marcus Garvey, served with the British West Indies Regiment during World War 1, entertaining troops in Palestine and Egypt. He moved to London from New York in 1934, returning there in 1941. Thus, three postcards in an envelope reveal the most interesting new fact to be found in all the correspondence.

I take the opportunity to list Hobson's Crowder letters here, with the barest detail, because I am in the fortunate position to be able to do so, but I am not free to transcribe them. In all likelihood the album may eventually be sold on to a research library or enter a new prolonged period of hibernation, away from inquisitive eyes, in another private collection. For the sake of completeness the two letters deposited with Texas are included in italic. Cunard's letters to Crowder are almost certainly not extant. Places, but not detailed addresses, are shown where known. Everything is handwritten, in ink, with a couple of pencil exceptions.

On learning of Crowder's death, Cunard wrote Charles Burkhart on 24 April 1955: "Henry made me—and so be it." （

Friday afternoon, postmark 21.9.28, Venice to Florence
letter and envelope incl. expressions of love, water damaged

Sunday, postmark 24.IX.28, Venice to Florence
letter and envelope incl. expressions of love

Tuesday, 3 P.M., not stamped, prob. delivered by hand, Venice to Venice
letter and envelope, apology for lapse of behaviour in reply to a letter
from Cunard

Thursday, postmark 26.X.1928, Paris to London
letter and envelope incl. expressions of love

12.07, 27 Oc 28, Paris to London
telegram, confirming letters received and sent

Sunday morning, 8.45, date unknown, location unknown
letter incl. expressions of love, water damaged

date unknown, location uncertain, poss. Chapelle Réanville
brief note

date unknown, location uncertain, poss. Chapelle Réanville
brief regretful note

date unknown, Paris to Chapelle Réanville
telegram incl. tells of brilliant opening with Victor present, i.e., Nancy's
cousin Victor Cunard

Sunday eve, 18.30, date unknown, location uncertain, prob. Chapelle
Réanville
letter incl. expressions of love

Monday Night, 10:0, location uncertain, prob. Chapelle Réanville
incl. expressions of love and talk of Anna, prob. Nancy's housekeeper

Saturday March 3, 34, prob. London to London
letter in which Crowder writes about Negro: An Anthology

postmark 17 Oct 1934, Dudley, Worcs. to London
three picture postcards of Dudley, with envelope, on which Crowder
writes that he has received a letter from his solicitor saying he will not be
granted a permit to work in England, that he has overstayed his visit, that
unless his manager can adjust this he will have to return to France, that
he will see Nancy on Sunday

Oct. 27 - 1953, Washington D.C. to Paris
letter and envelope incl. about Ezra Pound and Norman Douglas

8 - 11 - 1954 [11 August], Washington D.C. to London
letter in which Crowder writes about Grand Man: Memories of Norman Douglas

11 - 29 - 54
Washington D.C. to poss. Lamothe-Fénelon, Lot
letter incl. about Washington, Marion Anderson, Norman Douglas

—

Henry Crowder, with Hugo Speck, *As Wonderful As All That? Henry Crowder's Memoir
of His Affair with Nancy Cunard, 1928–1935* (Navarro, CA, Wild Trees Press, 1987)

Anthony Barnett, *Listening for Henry Crowder: A Monograph on His Almost Lost Music*
(Lewes, E. Suss., Allardyce Book, 2007), incl. extensive bibliography and CD
updated at www.abar.net/crowder.htm

With grateful thanks to David Deiss, Christie's, Harry Ransom Research Center
Anne Chisholm, John Cowley, Konrad Nowakowski, Howard Rye, Val Wilmer

NANCY and HENRY
album designed by P L Martin, 1971
black, white, silver, two shades of grey, double C motif on both covers
courtesy David Deiss, photo Christie's

A Childe is
an anonym

Caroline Clark is a poet back in Lewes after Moscow and Montreal; Agenda published *Saying Yes in Russian* in 2012; she translated Olga Sedakova's "In Praise of Poetry", Open Letter, 2014; she contributed to *Snow, 3*

Kelvin Corcoran is an English poet whose most recent book is *Sea Table*, Shearsman, 2015; details of other books and activities, incl. musical collaborations, can be found at his author page at www.shearsman.com

Michael Farrell is an Australian poet raised in Bombala, living in Melbourne, whose books include *ode ode Salt*, 2002, *BREAK ME OUCH*, 3 Deep, 2006, *a raiders guide*, 2008, *open sesame*, 2012, *Cocky's Joy*, 2015, all Giramondo

Ksenia Golubovich is a Russian writer, philologist, editor, translator, living in Moscow, whose books, in Russian, include *Personae: Poems in Prose*, 2002, *Serbian Parables*, 2003, *Wishes Granted*, 2005

Nicky Hamlyn is a London-based film maker with fifty film, video, installation works over the last forty years; his book *Film Art Phenomena* appeared from BFI/Palgrave Macmillan in 2003 - www.nickyhamlyn.com

Takashi Hiraide is a Japanese poet, novelist, publisher; translated: *The Guest Cat*, New Directions, Picador, 2014 *For the Fighting Spirit of the Walnut*, ND, 2008, *Postcards to Donald Evans*, Tibor de Nagy, 2003 - www.takashihiraide.com

Isai Kalashnikov (1931–1980) Russian novelist born in Buryatia in the former Soviet Union whose epic *Zhestoki Vek*, about Genghis Khan, first appeared in 1978, from which our extracts, the first in English, are taken

Kumiko Kiuchi is a Tokyo-based Beckett scholar who has published Beckett-related articles incl. in *Snow, 2* she co-translated Paul de Man's *Blindness and Insight*; in 2015 she introduced Patrick Keiller's films to Japan

Joe Luna is the author of *Astroturf & Other Poems*, 2013, *Ten Zones*, 2014, both Hi Zero, *The Future*, Iodine, 2015 he lives and works in Brighton where he organizes Hi Zero readings - http://hizeroreadings.tumblr.com

Nico Luoma is a Helsinki-based artist who studied photography in Boston; work in a.o. Finnish National Gallery; recent expos Atlas Gallery, London, 2014, Gallery Taik Persons, Berlin, 2015 - www.nikoluoma.net

Mara Malanova is a Leningrad-born, in 1970, poet who grew up in Ulan-Ude and now lives in Moscow; her two books, in Russian, are *Express*, 2002, and *Vernacular*, 2006

D S Marriott is the author of several books incl. *The Bloods*, Shearsman, 2011, *In Neuter*, Equipage, 2013, and as David Marriott, *Haunted Life: Visual Culture and Black Modernity*, Rutgers UP, 2007; he contributed to *Snow, 1*

Mandy Pannett is the author of a novella *The Onion Stone*, Pewter Rose, 2011, and five collections of poetry incl. *All the Invisibles*, SPM, 2012, and *Jongleur in the Courtyard*, Indigo Dreams, 2015 - www.mandypannett.co.uk

Kat Peddie is first a poet whose work has appeared in *Tears in the Fence*, *Molly Bloom*, *Litmus*; her first pamphlet is *Spaces for Sappho*, Oystercatcher, 2016; she co-edits *ZONE* and is setting up a press with Canterbury's Free Range

Francis Ponge (1899–1988) French poet noted particularly for *Le Parti pris des choses*, 1942, and *La Fabrique du pré*, 1971; the only other translation of *Le Savon*, as *Soap*, by Lane Dunlop, first appeared from Cape in 1969

Lewis Porter is a New York pianist, and composer for jazz combo, saxophone concertos, string quartet he is the author of *John Coltrane: His Life and Music*, Michigan UP, 1998 - www.youtube.com/user/Lrpjazz

Ari Poutiainen is a Finnish violinist and composer, with duet CD with *Snow*, 3 contributor Stefano Pastor *North South Dial*, Slam, 2011; he is author of *Stringprovisation: A Fingering Strategy for Jazz Violin Improvisation*, 2009

Miklós Radnóti (né Glatter 1909–1944) Hungarian poet and literary translator, beaten for "scribbling" and executed on a forced march, whose last poems were discovered in his coat pocket when he was exhumed

Georges Rodenbach (1855–1898) Paris-resident Belgian poet and author of *Bruges-la-Morte*, 1892, twice trans. Wilfion, 1986, repr. U Scranton, 2007; Daedelus, 2005, depicting Bruges, the dead city, as a state of the soul

David Rose is a novelist, living just outside West London, who has published *Vault*, Salt, 2011 a collection of stories *Posthumous Stories*, Salt, 2013, and a second novel *Meridian*, Unthank, 2015

Alexandra Sashe is a poet living in Vienna; her collection *Antibodies* appeared from Shearsman in 2013 shaped by four cultures and languages today she names her cultural identity with the one word Christian

Victor Segalen (1878–1919) French naval doctor, archaeologist, poet, trans. works include *Paintings*, *René Leys* *Stèles* about which see "Victor Segalen", in Anthony Barnett, *Antonyms Anew: Barbs & Loves*, Allardyce Book, 2016

Gavin Selerie is a London poet whose books include *Hariot Double*, Five Seasons, 2016, *Music's Duel: New and Selected Poems*, Shearsman, 2009, *Le Fanu's Ghost*, Five Seasons, 2006, *Roxy*, West House, 1996

Mark Somos is an intellectual historian, Lecturer in Political Science at Yale University, Visiting Scholar at Harvard's Department of Government, and Senior Visiting Research Fellow in Law at University of Sussex

Will Stone is a poet, essayist, translator moving between UK and the continent; his translations include Nerval, Trakl, Roth, Zweig, Verhaeren; his first poetry collection *Glaciation* appeared from Salt in 2007

Lola Thomas is a photographer from Lewes, recently graduated, who continues to develop her images in her Brighton-based darkroom; she contributed to *Darwin*, 7, and online *Landscape Stories*, *Phases* - www.lola-thomas.com

Juliet Troy is an Anglo-Guyanese poet living in Hertforshire whose work includes *Rhythm of Furrows across a field*, Kater Murr, 2013, and *Motherhood*, Knives, Forks and Spoons, 2015

Robert Walser (1878–1956) Swiss writer, often in a microscript shorthand, of novels and stories, whose other translators have included Christopher Middleton, who first introduced him into English, and Susan Bernofsky

James Wilson is the author of prose poem collections *All the Colours Fade*, *The Song Remains the Same*, Hippocrene 2012, a novel *Three Bridges*, Neverland, 2014, he contributed to *Snow*, 1, 2, and is an editor at Swedenborg Society

Snowb(o)ard

Anthony Barnett is the author of collected *Poems &* and *Translations*, both Tears in the Fence
in assoc. Allardyce Book ABP, 2012, and collected critical essays *Antonyms Anew: Barbs & Loves*
Allardyce Book ABP, 2016; other books include bio-discographies of Stuff Smith and Eddie South
with violinistic CD series, and *Listening for Henry Crowder: A Monograph on His Almost Lost Music*, 2007
InExperience and UnCommon Sense in Translation, 2014, is a lecture delivered at Meiji University
works-in-progress *Gullible's Troubles, or, A Disaccumulation of Knowledge* and *The Making of a Story*

Ian Brinton is editor of an 80th birthday Jeremy Prynne festschrift, *For the Future*, Shearsman, 2016
A Manner of Utterance: The Poetry of J H Prynne, Shearsman, 2009, *An Andrew Crozier Reader*, Carcanet, 2012
Andrew Crozier, *Thrills and Frills: Selected Prose*, Shearsman, 2013; other books include *Contemporary Poetry:
Poets and Poetry Since 1990*, CUP, 2009; he is reviews editor at *Tears in the Fence*; his Bonnefoy and other
Ponge translations are published by Oystercatcher; he has written a history of the phenomenon of
a school, so to speak, of poets who came out of Dulwich College, which will be published soon

Fiona Allardyce

is an art restorer, specializing in frescos, who drew our snogo; she co-published
the first collected volumes of J H Prynne, *Poems*, Andrew Crozier, *All Where Each Is*
Douglas Oliver, *Kind*, and Veronica Forrest-Thomson, *Collected Poems and Translations*

SETTING NOTE

Your compositor AB©omposer does not like Roman type inserted into italic passages
so, with the permission of the relevant contributors, backward slanting italic *is used instead*